IT HAPPENED
in the
CATSKILLS

IT HAPPENED
in the
CATSKILLS

An Oral History in the Words of
Busboys, Bellhops, Guests,
Proprietors, Comedians, Agents,
and Others Who Lived It

Myrna Katz Frommer
and Harvey Frommer

HARCOURT BRACE JOVANOVICH, PUBLISHERS

SAN DIEGO   NEW YORK   LONDON

HBJ

Copyright © 1991 by Harvey and Myrna Frommer

Library of Congress Cataloging-in-Publication Data
Frommer, Myrna.
It happened in the Catskills; an oral history in the words of
busboys, bellhops, guests, proprietors, comedians, agents,
and others who lived it/Myrna Katz Frommer and Harvey
Frommer. — 1st ed.
p.   cm.
Includes bibliographical references and index.
ISBN 0-15-105210-7
1. Catskill Mountains (N.Y.) — Social life and customs.
2. Resorts — New York (State) — Catskill Mountains —
History — 20th century. I. Frommer, Harvey. II. Title.
F127.C3K37   1991
974.7'38 — dc20   90-40057

Designed by Lydia D'moch

Printed in the United States of America
First edition
A B C D E

PRECEDING PAGES

The Concord in the 1940s — a grand
façade, manicured lawns, and
Olympic-size swimming pool.

In loving memory of Abe and Gussie Katz.
They are a part of this story, too.

CONTENTS

A simple pleasure on a sunny afternoon: rowing on Kutsher's lake.

INTRODUCTION

This is the story of an area of about 250 square miles, approximately an hour and a half drive northwest of New York City, which over the course of this century became a resort phenomenon unlike any other.

Its beginnings were simple, inauspicious. Some Jewish immigrants from Eastern Europe, a few out of the multitudes that came to New York between 1880 and the First World War, left the Lower East Side of Manhattan and moved up to the farmlands of the southwestern Catskill Mountains in Sullivan and Ulster counties. The area had attracted tourists since the post–Civil War years, drawing its appeal from its scenic vistas and accessibility from New York City via two railroad lines, the Ontario & Western and the Ulster & Delaware. The new arrivals, however, came up to the Mountains for more than a visit. They looked to settle, to farm, to escape the unhealthy environment of tenement life.

The names of Catskill towns evoke an America of another day.

Swiftly the message came back to the Lower East Side: the scenery was beautiful, the air was fresh and clean, the climate in July and August was pleasant. So landslayt—people from the same region in Europe—began coming up to spend a summer week or two. Farmhouses turned into summer boardinghouses as visitors arrived seeking simple pleasures: a meal of farm-fresh foods, a stroll down a shady lane, a midafternoon nap on a grassy lawn, a nice view from a gazebo or veranda.

After World War I, boardinghouses multiplied. Many evolved into hotels and clusters of cottages called bungalow colonies, and the region became a quasi-official vacation site for thousands of Jews from New York City and its environs. In its heyday, as many as 500 resorts catered to visitors of varied interests and incomes. The evolution of the region, especially of those resorts that grew elaborate and luxurious, mirrored—even crystallized—a twofold process: the Americanization of the Jewish population on the one hand, and the impact of Jewish culture on America on the other.

Vacation itself was an entirely novel concept, an American idea, to a population that had been historically impoverished and oppressed. But as American Jews began relaxing in their newfound freedoms and enjoying, for once, the fruits of their labors, pleasures once decidedly reserved for "yenem"—others—seemed within reach.

The Catskill resorts reflected this changed perception, as the active, conscious, and organized pursuit of pleasure came to define the burgeoning region. In the early years, nostalgic reminders of "di alte heym"—the old country—were enough: berry patches for picking, a lake or pond for bathing and boating, some klezmer tunes played on a piano and fiddle. Later, games learned on city streets or in schoolyards, like handball, basketball, and baseball, were transplanted to vacation settings, and hired entertainers bridged the transition from the Old World to the New with a repertoire of both Yiddish and American songs and inside humor. Before long, however, greater prosperity and notions of leisure-class activities demanded "all-American" facilities: tennis courts, swimming pools, golf courses. Winter sports, indoor pools and tennis courts, nightclub entertainment by leading stars in show business: these, too, came to resorts located just outside of little towns whose names—Ferndale, Woodridge, Monticello, Liberty—evoked an America of another day.

At the same time, Jewish culture was making its mark on American life. A legion of comedians had grown up in the neighborhoods of Manhattan, Brooklyn, and the Bronx. Their humor, anchored in the shtetls, may have been sharpened by the crassness of freewheeling life on street corners and outside of candy stores. Their shtik, delivered in the nasal cadences of New York Jewish speech, may have debuted on the vaudeville circuit and in Coney Island saloons. But they were nursed and nurtured and cut their teeth in Catskill resorts. It was in Fallsburg and Ellenville, in Mountain Dale and Swan Lake and other Catskills towns that these vigorous comedians delivered their particular view of life—with its pathos, irony, self-mockery, sarcasm, and vulgarity—that would via radio, movies, and television reach the nation at large. So was America informed about the Jewish mother, the insatiable Jewish appetite, the anxieties, foibles, and feats of the American Jew. But by then, as Lenny Bruce used to say, you didn't have to be Jewish to be Jewish.

The Catskill resorts of the 1990s are a paradox. Of the hundreds that once existed, little more than a dozen remain, yet these thrive. They are modern, attractive, complete in offerings, continuing the tradition of the all-inclusive vacation package innovated in the Catskills and only later picked up by cruises and Club Med–type enterprises. They remain steeped in their Jewish heritage yet frequently cater to a Gentile crowd. A kosher Friday night dinner in the Concord dining room ends with a priest delivering a benediction "in the name of the Father and of the Son and of the Holy Spirit" to a Knights of Columbus gathering. The Pines' yearly bluegrass festival brings a crowd from West Virginia, Tennessee, and Kentucky. Groups of senior

LEFT: The Nevele in an aerial view, 1989 — ultramodernity in a bucolic valley. RIGHT: An idyllic postcard vision of the Nevele in the 1930s.

citizens flock to the Paramount from Ohio and Pennsylvania as often as from New York.

The appeal of Catskill resorts has expanded even beyond national boundaries. So many Japanese golfers play the Concord's renowned Monster course that information in the clubhouse restaurant is printed in Japanese. Dressed to the nines and dead serious about their game, they demur when asked whether they mind not having sushi on the menu. "We like bagels and lox," they affirm, take our photograph, and politely excuse themselves. It is nearly time for dinner, they say, and Dionne Warwick is appearing in the Imperial Room afterward.

How these things came to be is the subject of this book. Told by those who lived it, this is a collection of recollections as old as the turn of this century and as new as its final decade. It contains the memories of busboys and bellhops, guests and chefs, singers and dancers, comedians and proprietors, bookers and agents, waiters and musicians—memories of nearly a century of life at a singular place. Together, they suggest a paraphrase of the lyrics from a song that was popular in the 1950s: there's a line between truth and memory that's sometimes hard to see, but it all leaves the very same sensation.

The closeness of the times: this group at Tamarack Lodge includes owner Dave Levinson (third from left), movie star Ilona Massey (third from right), and football great Allie Sherman (far left).

CAST OF CHARACTERS

JIMMY ABRAHAM

has been a waiter at the Concord Hotel since 1967. His popularity with famous guests has earned him the nickname Celebrity Jimmy.

JOEY ADAMS

comedian and syndicated columnist, began his show business career in the Catskills.

MARTY ALLEN

has appeared on television and in live performances all over the world. He is half of the comedy team of Allen and Rossi.

AL ALTIERI

is a New York City music teacher who for many years has been an orchestra leader at the Concord.

MOREY AMSTERDAM

star of television and movies, is affectionately remembered by television audiences for his role as Buddy on "The Dick Van Dyke Show."

SAM ANDIMAN

is a former teacher who tended bar in various Catskill hotels during the 1950s.

VIC ARNELL

came to the Catskills in 1954 and began his career as a comedian at the Swan Lake Hotel.

FREIDA BAKER

has been the orchestra leader at the Paramount Hotel since 1956.

FLORA BERGER

is a retired New York City schoolteacher who spent many summers as a guest at Catskill hotels.

MARNIE BERNSTEIN

is the pseudonym of a free-lance writer who remembers a special summer at a small Catskill resort.

CHARLES BRETT

a stockbroker who claims he has played every golf course in the Mountains, first visited the Catskills in 1919 when he was seven.

KERMIT BUCKTER

was maitre d' at Brown's Hotel for more than three decades.

MIKE CASTELUZZI

is the director of golf operations at the Concord.

IRVING COHEN

has the longest tenure of any maitre d' in the Catskills, having been at the Concord for nearly half a century.

BERNIE COVE

was maitre d' at the Pines Hotel for many years. He appeared in the movie *Sweet Lorraine*.

NORM CROSBY

is a satirist who regularly appears on television and the nightclub circuit.

ERROL DANTE

a nightclub and Catskill singer, is a longtime observer of the Catskill scene.

STEVE DELLA

started out as a musician at the Concord and went on to become the hotel's director of entertainment.

ART D'LUGOFF

is the proprietor of the Village Gate in Greenwich Village. As a college student, he worked as a busboy in Catskill hotels.

JACK EAGLE

is known for his portrayal of Brother Dominic in the Xerox commercial. He has appeared at Catskill resorts as comic and trumpet player for over half a century.

BILLY ECKSTINE

the fabled blues singer, was one of the first black performers to headline in the Catskills.

HARRIET EHRLICH

runs the family-owned Pines Hotel, founded by her parents, Phil and May Schweid.

JERRY EHRLICH

is married to Harriet Ehrlich and runs the Pines with her.

JAMES V. FARINA

a Cordon Bleu–trained chef, was head chef and director of food services at the Concord.

SHIMON FARKAS

was born in Hungary and was a practicing cantor in Sydney, Australia, for fifteen years. He is the cantor for the High Holy Days and Passover at the Concord.

BILLY FEIGENBAUM

is an Emmy Award–winning television graphic designer and the head of Feigenbaum in the Limelight.

BOB FELDMAN

for many years was the nightclub maitre d' at Brown's.

ELLIOT FINKEL

a musician and musical director who has performed in theaters on and off Broadway and throughout the country, developed his craft as a young man summering in Catskill hotels.

HARRY FIRST

is a New York City attorney who initially visited Grossinger's as a serviceman during World War II.

LEE FIRST

is a New York State judge and the wife of Harry First. The Firsts have visited Catskill resorts for over thirty years.

DAVID FISHER

a native Israeli who has been a cantor in Israel and South Africa, is the cantor at Kutsher's for the High Holy Days and Passover. He has played the role of Jean Valjean in the Israeli production of *Les Misérables*.

EDDIE FISHER

one of America's alltime favorite crooners, was "discovered" in the Catskills. His voice continues to "bring back the thrill."

BARRY FOX

is the longtime nightclub manager at the Nevele.

BARRY FRANK

whose entertaining days go back to children's radio shows, began his Catskill connection in 1959 at the Laurels Country Club. Now he is master of ceremonies, talent booker, and resident tummler at the Raleigh Hotel.

MORTY FRANKEL

has experienced the entire range of Catskill accommodations from boarding houses to resort hotels. He is currently a businessman who lives on Long Island.

NAOMI PARKER FRIEDMAN

is the granddaughter of Arthur Winarick, founder of the Concord.

FRED GASTHALTER

owns and operates the Paramount Hotel, founded by his grandfather.

MAX GOLDBERG

as a youth, played the clarinet for pennies throughout the Catskills.

LOU GOLDSTEIN

social director at Grossinger's for many years, is a television personality who regularly stumps audiences with his rendition of Simon Sez.

RALPH GREENBERG

is a former Long Island University basketball player. Today he operates a concession at Tamarack Lodge.

JOEY GREENWALD

son of the late Phil Greenwald, talent booker at the Concord, is a New York City stockbroker.

PAUL GROSSINGER

son of Jennie and Harry Grossinger, founders of Grossinger's Hotel, ran the hotel with his sister Elaine Etess for many years. He died in March 1989.

TANIA GROSSINGER

wrote *Growing Up at Grossinger's*. She is a freelance writer and public relations consultant.

MIKE HALL

is a New York press agent whose clients include film companies and book publishers. As a youth, he was simultaneously busboy, waiter, and writer of the daily paper at Grossinger's before graduating to the Concord dining room.

LIONEL HAMPTON

the world-renowned jazz musician, conductor, and composer, first played in the Catskills in the 1940s.

NORMAN HANOVER

is a professor of history at the City University of New York who remembers a special kind of education at the Pineview Hotel in Fallsburg.

ERNIE HARING

a retired customs officer, was a busboy at Grossinger's in the late 1930s and early 1940s.

LINDA HOPKINS

star of such Broadway shows as *Purlie, Me and Bessie Smith*, and *Black and Blue*, has a special affection for the Catskills, where she has frequently entertained.

JACKIE HORNER

who taught dance at Grossinger's for over twenty years, is a dance and aerobics instructor at Catskill hotels and colleges. She is married to Lou Goldstein.

CEIL BECKMAN JACOBS

was a singer and dancer on the vaudeville circuit. She was married to the late Al Beckman, talent booker and partner in Beckman and Pransky.

DICK KITTRELL

is a New York attorney and frequent Catskill visitor.

ROBERT KOLE

performed on Broadway in many musicals, including *West Side Story*. He lives in the Catskills where he has entertained for many years.

JEFF KROLICK

has been performing in the Catskills since he was thirteen. He is currently the Nevele's orchestra leader.

HELEN KUTSHER

is married to Milton Kutsher and is the hostess at Kutsher's Hotel.

MILTON KUTSHER

owns and operates Kutsher's Hotel, a resort he began and developed in the years following World War II.

MAL Z. LAWRENCE

calls the Catskills "my Hollywood." The Bronx-born comedian is a perennial favorite with Catskill audiences.

NORMAN LEIGH

has been the entertainment booker and master of ceremonies at the Nevele for many years.

PHIL LESHIN

former musician and now publicist, vividly recalls his summer of 1942 in the Catskills.

DAVE LEVINSON

is the former owner of Tamarack Lodge, founded by his parents.

BOB LIPMAN

is a publicist and longtime observer of the Catskill scene.

DICK LORD

is a Brooklyn-born comedian who has made hundreds of appearances
at Catskill resorts.

ELAINE MARKSON

is a New York City literary agent whose youthful Catskill experiences helped
inspire the idea for this book.

TONY MARTIN

one of the first big stars to appear at the Concord, has been a major recording
artist and concert singer for decades.

BOB MELVIN

is a comedian who has worked in the Catskills for many years.

JOSEPH "PICKLES" MERGLIANO

acquired his nickname working for Ziskind's Smokehouse in Monticello.
He has been both a limo driver and bellman for Catskill resorts.

SANDI MERLE

is a New York publicist who was long associated with the Brickman Hotel.

ROBERT MERRILL

the Metropolitan Opera star, affectionately remembers how his Depression
days' experiences in the Catskills honed his performing skills.

BEN PAISNER

was for many years the band director and manager at Sha Wan Ga Lodge.

GEORGE PARKER

is the grandson of Arthur Winarick, founder of the Concord. He is managing
director and CEO of that hotel.

ROBERT PARKER

former president of the Concord, is the grandson of Arthur Winarick.

SHARON PARKER

is director of guest relations and official hostess of the Concord. She is married
to George Parker.

JOHNNY PRANSKY

is half of the Beckman and Pransky talent-booking agency. He is now retired
and living in New Jersey.

HOWARD RAPP

is a partner with Arnold Graham in Charles Rapp Enterprises, the talent-booking agency founded by his uncle, Charlie Rapp.

SAL RICHARDS

came to the Catskills in 1972 after working the "Boccie Belt" as a comedian for several years.

ARTHUR RICHMAN

former New York City sportswriter and current media-relations director for the New York Yankees, pioneered the practice of bringing major league baseball players to the Catskills.

DAVID RICHTER

a podiatrist who lives on Long Island, has been a frequent guest at Catskill resorts.

CHASKELE RITTER

is a world-famous cantor whose home base is Temple Hillel in North Woodmere, New York. His Catskill experience includes roles as guest and cantor.

MAC ROBBINS

is a popular comedian who began his Catskill association as an athletic director at the Sunrise Manor Hotel in 1939. He was featured in the film *Punchline*.

FREDDIE ROMAN

well-known comedian on the nightclub circuit, began his career over thirty years ago at Homowack Lodge. He was featured in the film *Sweet Lorraine*.

STEVE ROSSI

is a partner in the comic team of Allen and Rossi and a familiar performer to audiences everywhere.

BERNIE ROTH

was the comptroller at Grossinger's and is currently general manager of Brown's.

PETER ROTHHOLZ

heads a public relations firm in Manhattan.

IRVING RUDD

raconteur and former public relations director for the Brooklyn Dodgers, is now publicist for Top Rank.

NIPSEY RUSSELL

the comedian, has performed hundreds of times in the Catskills.

DAVID BRENNER
Labor Day Weekend

ALAN "BLACKIE" SCHACKNER

is a renowned harmonica player who has appeared on concert stages world-
wide. He began his career in 1938 as a member of the social staff
at Young's Gap.

MARVIN SCOTT

is an Emmy Award–winning journalist and a television news anchor in
New York City. He was once a bellhop at the Raleigh Hotel.

LEBA SEDAKA

is married to Neil Sedaka and functions as his manager. She grew up in
Monticello spending the summers at Esther Manor, which was owned and
operated by her mother, Esther Strassberg.

NEIL SEDAKA

is a well-known singer, pianist, and composer. He has never forgotten his
nineteenth summer as a member of the Nordanelles at Esther Manor.

JACK SEGAL

is a former talent booker and the founder of PEP Shows. Now retired,
he makes his home in New Jersey.

RUTH SELTZER

spent about ten summers in the Catskills. Today she is a housewife who lives
on Long Island.

ARTHUR SHULMAN

grew up in Liberty, New York, and now resides in Washington, D.C., where
he is communications director for B'nai Brith International.

SHELLY SHUSTER

used to run the bar at Esther Manor together with his partner, Joe Childs.
Today they operate several New York City eateries.

JULIE SLUTSKY

is the former owner of the Nevele, which was founded by his father. His
golden moments include rooting for Nevele Pride.

BILL SMITH

is the historian for the Sullivan County Historical Association.

THERA STEPPICH

is a native of Germany, where she was an Olympic Games gymnast in the
1930s. She is a longtime front desk person at the Concord.

STEWIE STONE

a Brooklyn-born and -bred comedian who attended Brooklyn College, claims that he majored in stickball.

ESTHER STRASSBERG

together with her sister Irene Asman, long ran and operated Esther Manor, the hotel founded by her father.

MIKE STRAUSS

was a sportswriter for the *New York Times* for over fifty years. His contact with the Catskills began in 1918, and he went on to write often about Catskill winter sports. He is now a sports columnist for the *Palm Beach Daily News*.

SETH THOMAS

decided on his current profession, performing musician, as a five-year-old guest at Kaminsky's Bungalow Colony.

SIMON TIMLICHMAN

is a choir director. He was born in the Ukraine and came to the United States in 1972.

ROBERT TOWERS

is the president of a Manhattan advertising agency whose accounts include the U.S. Open, the Nevele, and the Concord. He is a legendary Catskill figure.

MICHAEL TRAGER

is a college student and works for a New York City hotel.

ALAN TRESSER

is the social director at the Fallsview Hotel and has been associated with the Catskills since 1937.

JERRY VALE

is an internationally known recording artist and performer who regularly sings in the Catskills.

GERALD VINCENT

is a young dancer who makes his home in Los Angeles.

BILLY VINE

is the technical director of entertainment at the Concord Hotel. He is the son of the late comedian Billy Vine, Sr.

JOAN WALTERS

is a talent manager and longtime observer of the Catskill scene.

JERRY WEISS

came to Grossinger's as a young refugee from Nazi Germany. He went on to become entertainment director at Grossinger's, a post he held for over thirty years.

MARVIN WELKOWITZ

spent his teenage summers at his parents' hotel, the Ridge Mountain.

STEVE WHITE

is director of tennis operations at the Concord and the grandnephew of Arthur Winarick, founder of the hotel.

GLORIA WINARICK

the wife of Gordon Winarick, first came to the Catskills with her father, the Yiddish actor Irving Grossman.

GORDON WINARICK

is the executive marketing director of the Concord Hotel and the nephew of Arthur Winarick, founder of the hotel.

SOL ZIM

has been cantor at Hollis Hills Synagogue in Queens for more than twenty-five years and is also half of the popular singing duo, the Brothers Zim.

IT HAPPENED
in the
CATSKILLS

Congregating outside the main building of Kutsher's Country Club in the 1940s.

PROLOGUE

ROBERT TOWERS: A hotel of the '20s, '30s: two hundred acres, a main building with a porch and dining room. Across the road a swimming pool and the playhouse. A generation of people who sat on rocking chairs, who waited to go from one meal to the next, whose idea of outdoor recreation was horseshoe pitching, or gossip in the dining room, or waiting for that show to go on at night. I'm talking about the Grossingers, the Slutskys with the Nevele, the Levinsons with Tamarack Lodge in Greenfield Park.

The closeness of those times. The guests were actually your house-guests. It was like having a relative for dinner, or a friend. There was such an empathy. People stayed the season. Got to know the staff. Got to know their shtik.

You'd get your crowd from New York, but then you'd get a guy from Burlington, Vermont, who ran the local dry goods store. He was one of yours. He had heard about it. He wanted to see it.

Social staffs had people like Moss Hart at the Flagler, or Neil Simon at Tamiment. They'd do scenes from plays like Kingsley's *Dead End* or Odets' *Waiting for Lefty* or musicals like the Garment Workers' *Pins and Needles*. The ambitious ones might do scenes from operas if a guy on the staff could sing an aria from *Pagliacci* or *The Barber of Seville*.

Game nights: apple bobbing, limbo dancing, Simon Sez—all the games we knew as kids. A handball court that said "Lake Mohegan Athletic Field"—that was the whole field.

There was a humor, an escape, a special feeling. It was a club, a sorority, a fraternity, a lodge. "Where'd you go last year?" You went to Grossinger's, you went to Paul's, you went to Young's Gap, White Roe, Avon Lodge, the President, the Windsor, the Ambassador, the Laurels . . .

ONE

A PLACE IN THE COUNTRY

BILL SMITH: The settlers came in the early nineteenth century on foot or by horse and wagon. Later on they took stagecoaches. When the O & W Railroad—the New York, Ontario & Western—came through in the 1870s and built a series of creameries and transported milk to New York City, the center part of Sullivan County opened up.

The Jews started arriving toward the end of the century. The men, who were farmers, would leave their wives and children on the farm for the winter. They'd go to the city, take any job that was available, and come back whenever they could. Sometimes they were away for

a whole winter. In the summer they would return. The lucky ones made contacts in the city and brought people up to summer in the country. Mothers would move children to outer housing, and the rest of the family would sleep wherever they could. The bed of the farmer and his wife would be given over to boarders. That's how the early people made a living. It was a survival net, a day-to-day thing for many of them.

JULIE SLUTSKY: My grandfather Charles Slutsky had been a farmer in Russia, so after he came to America he went to Ulster County with his wife and family to buy a farm. Little by little they began taking in boarders over the summer and buying up adjoining property. You find the same story all over the Mountains, except ours is the oldest existing hotel in the entire area. Our roots stretch back to 1901.

Life back then was very hard. My grandfather and my father dug cellars and sold firewood—anything to stay afloat. In the winters my father worked in an umbrella factory in New York City. For years the people from the umbrella factory came up as guests.

One day when my father, Joseph, was grown and ready to be on his own, my grandfather suggested they divide the property. "Take whichever side you want," my father said.

"No, you make the choice," my grandfather insisted.

So my father selected the site of the present Nevele Hotel, and my grandfather's site became the Fallsview. There is a waterfall on the Nevele property. Years ago, eleven schoolteachers were picnicking by the falls, and they decided to name it for the number of their group spelled backward. That's how "Nevele" came about. The Fallsview got its name because you can see the falls from that hotel.

My brother Ben and I grew up on the property and attended a one-room schoolhouse that today stands on the Nevele grounds. I used to walk to school through the fields.

Two exclusive resorts used to exist in the area when I was a kid. One was called Mt. Meenahga House—the Indian word for huckleberry—and it was 1,200 feet above Ellenville. The place was built on 100 acres in 1881 by a man named Terwilliger. It had miles and miles of walks and drives, lots of laurel, sweetbrier, and wild flowers. Mt. Meenahga was restricted to Gentiles and catered to the carriage trade. Then around 1920, a Jewish family named Kurtz that made its money in the cloak-and-suit business bought the place. The Nevele was pretty well established by then, and we would stage band competitions in Ellenville with them.

Of all the places in Ulster County when I was a kid, Yama Farm was probably the most elegant. I believe President Wilson stayed there when he visited the Catskills after World War I. I saw him coming through the region with a brigade of security people.

Guests came up to Yama Farm in chauffeur-driven limousines and paid up to $100 a day for a cottage and servants. That was unheard of in the 1920s. Tammany people from New York City were frequent guests. Governor Al Smith stayed there; his daughter and her husband went there for their honeymoon.

But the Nevele was far from luxurious. Ben and I were brought up in the hard school. We were a working farm until 1938, and Ben and I did our share of chores. We furrowed the fields, picked crops, milked cows. The local boys who worked in the summers as waiters used to go out to the fields in their uniforms to pitch hay and then come back into the dining room. As hard as they tried, they could never quite brush off every last piece of hay from their uniforms. Ben

LEFT: The trip by car from New York City could take up to eight hours — and that was good time. These drivers made it up to the Nevele in the winter. RIGHT: The old Nevele in a winter setting.

and I worked in the hotel too—busboys, waiters, maintenance work—whatever had to be done, we did.

ESTHER STRASSBERG: My parents, Philip and Dora Goldstein, came from Russia and Poland, and my father worked as a designer of men's clothing in New York City. My mother used to tell us how she would put her baby in the carriage outside, and the cinders from the elevated trains would fall all over it. She kept asking my father to get her a place in the country.

My father read an advertisement in a Jewish newspaper about farms for sale in Monticello. So he went up there with a partner (whom he later bought out), and they found a farm and boardinghouse on 200 acres. It was owned by a man named John Hill and his son Arthur, and it catered to a Gentile crowd of what we used to call the "intelligentsia." They named the place the Beauty Maple House, and it opened for business in 1904. It was the first Jewish boardinghouse in the area.

We were a large family, five boys and two girls, and we all grew up in Monticello and went to the one-room schoolhouse in School District Number 6. I still remember seeing signs in Ferndale that said JEWS NOT ALLOWED. And nobody ever threw the signs down.

ARTHUR SHULMAN: There was anti-Semitism in the area; Jews were in the minority. Yet there was ambivalence because the Gentiles made a lot of money from the resort trade. Immigrant and first-generation American Jews banded together in the Catskills, and they felt comfortable there. There was really no other place to go for vacations, because so many places were restricted. We were in the Catskills because my father had tuberculosis, and the area with higher elevation had a reputation for TB cures. He got up there around 1929.

FRED GASTHALTER: My father, Sam, was six years old in 1906, when he came up to Parksville with his father, a hat maker from New York City, who suffered from TB. Parksville, Ferndale, Liberty—those towns are higher than most of Sullivan County. The Town of Liberty was known for its sanitariums, including the famous Loomis and Workmen's Circle sanitariums. Naturally, the hotels didn't want the stigma of anything connected to TB, so they distanced themselves from the Liberty post office. Grossinger's and Young's Gap were both in Liberty, but Grossinger's said they were in Ferndale, and Young's Gap said they were in Parksville.

We were the second Jewish family in Parksville. My grandfather bought a small farm and a few years later started taking in boarders. Some people complained the altitude in Parksville was too high for them. It's 1,670 feet, which is just 100 feet higher than the neighboring towns. I still get that argument. Maybe they're afraid of getting nosebleeds. I tell them, "Check it out with your doctor—provided he's under eighty years old."

By 1920, my grandfather had passed away, and my father was running the place by himself. He named the place the Paramount from the Paramount Theatre in Manhattan.

Parksville became a big hotel area; there were so many of them along Route 17. Young's Gap was probably the most famous of them all. In the late 1920s, it had an indoor pool, a gym, a ballroom, and room for 400 guests.

ESTHER STRASSBERG: In the 1920s, many of the boardinghouses expanded into hotels. By 1929, twenty-five years after he opened the Beauty Maple House, my father had to decide whether to expand or give up. He decided to expand. You know what that means: boarders become guests and prices go up. We could no longer charge $18 a week including three meals a day.

We remodeled so that we could cater to 550 people. We added the things hotels had, like nice public rooms and a social staff, and we changed the name. My father decided to call the hotel after me, the first daughter after five boys. That's how we became Esther Manor.

We also bought little bungalow colonies on all sides of us, so we would know who our neighbors would be. And the bungalow renters were entitled to use all of the Esther Manor facilities, watch all the entertainment. And for a little extra they could eat in our dining room.

Before they came up for the summer, they had to give us a deposit of half their rental. Before they took occupancy, they paid the balance. In this way we got capital to fix up and maintain the place before the season. We didn't have to borrow from the banks. A lot of other people had trouble getting loans and paying back with interest. Many couldn't make the payments. We never had that problem.

BILL SMITH: The resorts in the Catskills always had problems borrowing money to put in improvements or just to stay afloat. Places kept expanding and the competition was intense. If one hotel put in an elevator, another put in two elevators. If one installed a swimming pool, another installed a larger pool. Success was a fickle thing—whether the season was good, whether the family made money. Some owners got tied up with money lenders at such high prices they couldn't meet the payments. Sometimes a large hotel held the mortgages on a few smaller places and eventually swallowed them up. Some people even leased out or rented their hotels for a season while doing other things, hoping to raise enough money to be able to come back and make their place a going proposition.

DAVE LEVINSON: Pop and Mom, Max and Dora Levinson, arrived at Greenfield Park, the present location of Tamarack Lodge, on January 3, 1900. They were born in Minsk, Russia, but had lived in New York since 1885. Pop was visiting some friends in Woodridge and thought it was healthier up there than in New York—the air was clean and good. So he bought a dairy farm of about fifty acres with about twenty-five cows and four horses.

At that time there were six girls in the family. (Later I came along and then two more girls.) Pop brought them all up here and went back to work as a tailor in New York. My sisters would complain to Mom: they thought Pop bought the farm for his health—so why was he in New York and they were here?

In 1903, Pop saw that his neighbors were making a living by catering to boarders, so he built six bedrooms, added on to the little house that they had, and went into the boardinghouse business. They charged $3.50 per person per week for all the milk you could drink, all the eggs you could eat, plus whatever meat you got fed. Whatever little profit he made went into more rooms, and that's how Tamarack grew.

Back in 1905, when the Ellenville National Bank was the Home National Bank, Pop went to borrow $500. Old man Cox, president of the bank, said, "Max, how long you a farmer?" Pop said, "About five years." Cox said, "It's about time you shouldn't need any money."

So Pop said, "Well, if you can't give me the money, I'll have to wait till the summer and pay my bills then instead of now. I don't like to be behind in my bills, but you're forcing me into it."

Lo and behold, at the end of the month the bank statement comes, and they'd made a mistake and gave Pop $800 too much money to his deposit. Pop went to the bank and withdrew the money.

A couple of weeks later, they discovered their mistake and called Pop down to the bank. They told him what happened.

Pop said, "Mr. Cox, I don't read English too well. I thought all that money was mine, and I spent it. All I can do now is give you a note for $800."

Well, they had no other choice. They took the note, and Pop paid it off. But that was how he got his credit established. He always got money after that.

Pop continued to be a dairy farmer even with the hotel.

He was an orthodox Jew but very liberal-minded. When I was about eight years old, Pop wanted me to learn Hebrew. There were no Jewish kids around at that time. I wouldn't sit down and study unless my friends, Olden Townsend and Oscar Newkirk, learned Hebrew with me. So Pop gave them a couple of pennies, and they studied with me. Later on Olden Townsend, who became a doctor, came up

An Ellenville scene in the post–Civil War years. The large building in the rear is the Delaware & Hudson Canal Company freight office.

here to visit, and he said to my father, "Mr. Levinson, let me see if I can still write my name in Jewish." And he was able to. Olden's grandfather, by the way, had been a colonel or general in the Civil War. I knew him. There were a lot of Civil War veterans around when I was a kid.

There was no telephone here in the early days, no electricity—they used kerosene lights. Of course there were no cars. We had a pair of mustangs, and my sister Daisy would drive them with an old dash wagon and would go racing down the country roads. The Gentile neighbors would cry out, "Daisy, you're gonna break your damn fool neck someday." Once those mustangs ran away from her, and she almost *was* killed.

Later on, our neighbor bought a Model T Ford, but come wintertime the car was jacked up and put away. Nobody plowed the snow. I'd go to school with a horse and sleigh, taking the milk down to the creamery with me.

We went to a one-room schoolhouse through the eighth grade. It had been around since the 1850s or maybe even before. In 1933, our schools became centralized, and the buses began to pick up the children. But the schoolhouse is still there with the two outhouses and the woodshed.

I was sixteen when we began building the main house in 1926. I was reading the blueprints. The architect and carpenter would call me at school to see if it was all right to make certain changes. And the principal would call me out of the classroom and say, "Dave, I think we'll have to put a telephone at your desk." I always felt tied to the hotel. A lot of the boys in Ellenville got out of school and they'd be on the streets, kibitzing around. But I wanted to get back. There was always something to do.

In 1929, a young woman came up on the O & W Railroad on a Friday night. I escorted her to her room. It was a dormitory with eighteen beds in the old casino, which we divided in half for boys and girls. She had reserved a room with a private bath and was very disappointed, but she stayed and had a good time. Still, she swore she'd never come back. So, in order not to lose a customer, I married her. That was my motto: "Never lose a guest."

Around the time we got married, we discontinued the farm. We were down to ten or twelve cows by then. I had begun to realize the smell of barn didn't leave me, and so I decided it was time to sell the cows.

Tamarack Lodge grew to 300 rooms, but I never wanted to be the Tiffany of the Mountains. We were the Woolworth's of the Mountains, and we were always full. God was good to us.

Pop died in 1948 at the age of ninety, but Mom lived until 1965 when she was ninety-four. She used to tell the story of her grandfather who on Simchath Torah—you know, the holiday where everybody has a feast and drinks a little—he drank a bit too much, and he sat down and cried that at the age of ninety-five he was an orphan.

My sister Rose, who passed away at the age of ninety-seven in June 1989, built the Stevensville Lake Hotel with our aunt and Harry Dinnestein in 1924. She had lost her husband at the time, and Pop thought it would be a good idea for her to go into the hotel business. He helped her out with it. They sold out to Harry in 1952. My sister Bess, who married a Sussman, ran the Kiamesha Country Club in Kiamesha Lake, and Jan Peerce was their band leader from 1928 to 1932.

I've been around long enough to remember them all: the Beerkill down the road—1905, the Nevele—1901, Grossinger's—1914, Morningside early 1900s after us, the Flagler Hotel in Fallsburg—1910 or so. We weren't the first boardinghouse in the area, but there weren't too many others when we came.

MIKE STRAUSS: I first came up to the Catskills in 1918, with the O & W Railroad, and getting up those mountains was tough. The train had two locomotives to drag you there. You'd come to Summitville, a turnoff point. From there a branch went northeast to Ellenville, heading toward Kingston, while the main line continued right on to Roscoe directly northwest.

MAX GOLDBERG: In the early days most people came up on the train. You had to close the windows all the way up because the soot would choke you. Farmers would pick you up at the station with a horse and wagon.

"Come to our place, it's the best!"

"Hey, come to ours, we're a real hotel!"

"I'm charging twelve dollars."

Along the O & W: the old Ferndale line. From here the train crossed a long, high bridge to Liberty.

"I'm charging thirteen, but with three delicious meals a day."
"Only fifteen dollars—best food, best view. Come with me!"
You listened. You went where you thought you'd get the best deal.

DAVE LEVINSON: Pop and I would pick up the guests at the railroad station with a horse and wagon. This was before there was a line to Ellenville. By the time the railroad stopped at Ellenville, there were taxis already—the Model T Fords, the Pierce-Arrows, the Chandlers, the Winstons. People ran jitney businesses and would take our guests to and from the station.

Then later on, around 1928, the Model A Ford came out, and people started coming in their own cars, driving up over the Wurtsboro Mountain. We were eighteen miles away, in Greenfield Park, a two-hour drive in those days.

MIKE STRAUSS: If you came on a Friday, it was bumper to bumper all the way from New York City to Wurtsboro. It could take you seven, eight hours making good time. As you went through Suffern, Tuxedo,

Chester, Goshen on those narrow two-lane highways, policemen with badges on their overalls would stop you if you went over fifteen miles an hour. However, the chances of going that fast were slim because of the heavy traffic.

Kids would stand at the base of the Wurtsboro Mountain, where there's a little creek. They would fill cans of water from the creek, and for a nickel or a dime, they'd throw water on the burning brakes as the cars came down the hill. Brakes burned much more easily in those times. There'd always be a pile of empty soup cans on the bank of the creek.

ROBERT MERRILL: When I began coming up to the Catskills in the 1930s, the trip could take a whole day. Cars always overheated, and we'd spend all that time filling the radiators. The hills were monstrous. Cars couldn't make it up. One summer I got as far as Wurtsboro Mountain, but then the car wouldn't go any further. I sold it for $40 and hitchhiked the rest of the way.

CHARLES BRETT: My earliest memory of the Mountains goes back to 1919, when I went up with my grandmother, my aunt, and two cousins. We took a ferry from downtown Manhattan to Weehawken, New Jersey, where we got the train. We stayed at a place called Eliyuchem, and the owner met us at the station in Mountain Dale with a wagon pulled by two big horses. Eliyuchem was about eleven miles from the station, and it took about an hour to get there. The area was very rural with only dirt roads. We called it a farm—it had chickens and cows—but there really wasn't any farming. For the entire summer, the rental cost $40 for the room that my grandmother and I shared.

In the great big kitchen, there was a large coal stove, and it was lit every morning ready for cooking. Everybody shared the big ice box—there were no refrigerators back then. Eliyuchem was a true kochalayn—literally "cook alone"—where guests shared a kitchen and cooked their own food. My grandmother would make a big pot of oatmeal, and everybody would sit at a long table covered with a patterned oilcloth. We'd have the oatmeal and possibly a soft-boiled egg. There were no reserved seats—the first place you got, you sat. After breakfast, while the adults cleaned up, the kids would run out and play. I loved to pick green apples and blueberries and just be free in the country.

Saturday nights we would go to a nearby hotel for Yiddish entertainment. Although I was American-born, we all spoke Yiddish most of the time. A popular entertainment then was the mock marriage where the man dressed up as the bride, and the woman dressed up as the groom. The so-called cantor would sing, "Ven mir giest arayn dos galikhel, vert zi shvangerik." What it meant was "When the golden liquid is poured in, she'll get pregnant." I didn't understand why everyone laughed hilariously.

The oldest memories remain the most vivid.

ROBERT TOWERS: About sixty years ago, there was a black man who called himself Mendel. He was a wandering musician who'd go around and play on the lawns.

MAX GOLDBERG: I started when I was twelve, walking from hotel to hotel with my father, playing music on the lawns, collecting pennies in a hat. I played the clarinet, and he played the drum. We walked from Woodridge to Fallsburg to South Fallsburg to Monticello to Liberty.

Then my father hired a horse and wagon. Horses eat too, so we had to work even harder. My parents spoke only Yiddish, and Yiddish songs—klezmer music—was what we played: "Di Zilberne Khasene," "Sheyn vi di L'vone," "Di Grine Kuzine." We played the bulgars, the freylekhs, the horas—lively music that they all danced to. The people gave me pennies and sometimes a nickel. At the end of a day, we had about $8, maybe $50 at the end of a week.

We rented a bungalow for the whole summer for $50. Most of the money that we made, my father sent to my mother in New York City. She had four more sons at home to feed.

While we played on the lawns, the boss would sometimes say, "Come in and play in the lobby." Then he would ask us to play in the dining room. There was always a piano there, and I'd play it. When we were inside the hotel, the boss would say, "It's not nice for you to go around and collect money. Let me make the collections. You go into the kitchen and eat." We ate whatever was brought back from the dining room. There was a lot of good food left over.

MIKE STRAUSS: Back in the 1920s people in the smaller hotels used to wait on the porch or out on the lawn for the arrival of local peddlers after lunch. They were the forerunners of the Good Humor Man, and they were one of the highlights of the day. They would come in a horse and buggy, stop in front of the hotel, and ring a handbell. Guests would come running out, yelling, "The ice cream man is here!" The peddlers sold ice cream out of a big wooden tub the size of a garbage pail. Three-flavored bricks cost a nickel.

BILL SMITH: Otto Hillig of Liberty was the big photographer in those early years. His camera had a chrome die that printed the name of a hotel on the print. Hillig sold more than 10,000 postcards to the hotels, which in turn sold them to guests. They'd send them to friends and relatives all over the country. It was a great form of cheap advertising.

RUTH SELTZER: In the late 1920s, my father would take me, my mother, and my sister up to Rubin's Farm in Liberty in his furniture truck. The truck had an open top and didn't go that fast. It seemed like it took us forever to get there.

After he brought us up, my father would go back to work in the city, but he'd come up most weekends to be with us. We stayed from the Fourth of July to Labor Day, and in those days it was very inexpensive.

A Catskill scene by Otto Hillig, famed early Catskill photographer.

Rubin's Farm was very small—only about fifty people. The owners spoke Yiddish and also English. They took a liking to me and taught me country things, like how to milk a cow. I'd drink the milk straight from the cow—it was warm and delicious. My sister would go, "Yuck, I'm going to vomit."

For a city kid, it was a wonderful experience. I had never seen a chicken or a cow before then. We would pick blueberries, blackberries, and raspberries and fill big straw baskets or tin pails. We'd bring them into the kitchen, and they would make pies and jams. Rubin's was a kochalayn, and we would eat family style at a table covered with blue-and-white-check oilcloth. Whoever heard of linens in those days?

We were near Grossinger's but we spent all our time on the farm. There was a real old-fashioned casino, actually a converted barn with a stage and seats.

MORTY FRANKEL: Spenser's Bungalow Colony in Phillipsport was run by Gentiles, but all the guests were Jewish. Back of the pastures, beyond the farms, were wide barge canals with cement walls. There was no water in them by the time we were there, and we kids would play all kinds of games in them.

We'd go to pick berries, and the grown-ups would warn us, "Don't get caught by the Mountain People up there." Sure enough, just like in the picture *Deliverance*, regular mountain people lived up there.

The "feel" of an old hotel: the original building of the Pines.

They all seemed so big, with long full beards, dressed in overalls. We'd be picking berries or exploring, and sometimes they'd come out. We'd run all the way down the mountain till we got back to Spenser's place.

One summer we went to a kochalayn in Mountain Dale. It was like a farm with little cottages, and people made their own entertainment at night. The owner was called Mighty Adam. He was a Jewish fellow with a beard and mane; he looked like a hermit. He used to entertain people by using his hand to pound nails through two-by-fours, and he would bite nails in half. Remember the wagon wheels that they had on farms? Adam would pick one up and hold it over his head. People would come from all around to see Mighty Adam.

CHASKELE RITTER: The Ridge Mountain Hotel in Parksville was a small hotel that my family and I went to during the Roaring Twenties. My grandfather was the ritual slaughterer there for many years. I remember the adults milking the cows and bringing the milk straight to the table. And when the chickens dropped their eggs, my father and his friends used to take them and eat them.

There was a little casino on the premises that we used as a synagogue on Saturdays. Leibele Waldman, a well-known cantor and my boyhood idol, was a guest at the hotel, and sometimes he sang for the crowd. Later on, when I became a well-known cantor myself, I often thought about hearing Leibele Waldman pray at that small hotel in Parksville.

FLORA BERGER: We spent several summers before the war at Hardin's Farm, off Route 17 in Ferndale. It was a working farm, with white buildings. The main house was surrounded by a brook, and there were beautiful hills all around. Mrs. Hardin was always in the kitchen. Mr. Hardin was the handyman, and their two daughters were the waitresses and chambermaids.

All the clientele were friends, Jewish, and mostly New York City schoolteachers. There were about twenty-four to thirty guests for the eight-week season. It was a family crowd with a lot of young children always running around.

You paid $12 a week per adult and $5 or $6 for children for a four-room cottage and three meals a day. The shower was outdoors in a wooden stall, and the water was cold. Meals were served in the dining room of the main house, and you ate at long tables, eight to

Scenes at a Swan Lake bungalow colony around 1940. Husbands came up for the weekends; wives stayed all summer.

ten at a table, family style. The food was good but quite simple, with very little variation. Desserts would be a plain sponge cake one night, a chocolate cake the next. My children would never drink the milk because it came right from the cows.

The guests made their own entertainment. To tell the truth, during the week, there was absolutely nothing to do. I could just scream from boredom. I'd go crazy from looking at the babbling brook and all of the trees. How many times can you play Mah-Jongg?

But on the weekends, when the men came up, it was different. The couples would get together, and the men would tell stories about their week of work. There would be a lot of jokes and hilarity.

What made Hardin's distinctive was that the owners were a black family. There was absolutely no prejudice. It was unusual for those days.

MAX GOLDBERG: The Flagler was top of the line. I stayed there once paying $17 a week on a due bill. You know what a due bill was? The hotel owed money to somebody for an advertisement. I gave the money to the guy who ran the ad, and he crossed off from the account: "The Flagler—I took off $17 . . . Goldbergs."

MIKE STRAUSS: The Flagler was originally a Gentile and genteel boardinghouse in Fallsburg that opened in the 1870s. It advertised spacious grounds and games like lawn tennis and croquet. Then two Jewish men bought it and made it the place to be throughout the 1920s.

Grossinger's was still growing up, and there was no Concord, when I came there with my family in 1918. The Flagler had eighty rooms, fifty baths, hot and cold water, a telephone in every room. On the main floor there was a big lobby, a sun parlor, and a writing room. It was the first hotel in the Mountains to have an elevator and one of the first in the country to have a stucco exterior. Most of the others were clapboard.

The Flagler also had a compact nine-hole golf course. But all you could do in the winter, as far as sports was concerned, was ice skate. I skated on the Neversink River when it was just glare ice right behind the hotel.

ROBERT TOWERS: In the hotels of the '20s and '30s, a resident social staff planned the nighttime activity. There would be a social director who would organize shows for each night, a blues singer, a dance team, a dramatic actor who did readings from plays, and a tummler— the porch clown who hung around with the guests during the day. He'd clown around by the pool, make jokes in the card room, do routines in the dining room. When he went on at night, they loved him—he was their own kid. (Eddie Cantor might sit back and ask, "So, what's so funny about him?")

JOHNNY PRANSKY: When Al Beckman and I started out as agents, we booked entire social staffs for the season. There was a small place in Greenfield Park owned by a woman named Mary Kanfer. Listen to the social staff that we booked for her: Red Buttons was the comedian. He got about $50 for the whole summer. Red was a cute little son of a gun, and he tummeled all over. Joey Adams was the social director, and Jules Dassin was on the dramatic staff. That Mary Kanfer sure got her money's worth!

JOEY ADAMS: Everybody began in the Mountains. The first hotel I appeared at was the Olympic Hotel because my uncle owned it. Then I worked in the Beerkill Lodge in the late '30s, heading an entertainment staff that included Robert Alda, Red Buttons, Frances Forbes, and Bill Castle. I got $15 a week because I was the head guy, but I

Alan "Blackie" Schackner outside his Loch Sheldrake bungalow with guest William Bendix. In 1940 the two appeared on Broadway in William Saroyan's *The Time of Your Life*.

was also a busboy. Robert Alda was getting $10 a week and worked as a waiter at the same time. Bill Castle, who became a Hollywood producer, got the same. Red Buttons got $5 a week. That was big money because we also made money as waiters, busboys, delivering things, working in the kitchen, cleaning the rooms.

There was no such thing as "star" or "entertainer." We had a job, and we just did the entertainment because we loved it. All the entertainers had a little something extra in them. They'd try out shtik without knowing they were trying it out.

I made fun of real things that were happening, conversations that I overheard.

You heard a woman say, "Close the window. It's cold outside."

"So if I close the window, will it be warm outside?"

The food, the weather, the atmosphere—when you heard what people were saying, you tried it out. I made my staff eat with the people, talk with them, dance with them. That's where we learned how.

In the Mountains, we could kid each other, roast each other. You'd pass someone and say hello, and he'd say "Is Joey angry at me?"

"Why?"

"He didn't insult me once."

Nowadays there's no such thing as ad-lib or instant humor. A guy walks on stage, he's ready. If someone says hello, he's got thirty answers prepared.

In the Catskills I learned how to mingle, to talk to people, not just do shows. We never thought of what it would become. We just enjoyed it, making humor out of all the situations.

ALAN "BLACKIE" SCHACKNER: My first contact with the Mountains was in the summer of 1938, when I was about twenty and a member of the social staff at Young's Gap Hotel. I was the novelty act. All the girls who worked there were called prima donnas. The comics were the comica. And any kind of musical act was called the novelty.

My salary for the season was $200 plus room and board with double portions. My job was to play the harmonica on show nights and do some acting when needed. I also had to take care of the swimming pool and dance with the guests.

I'm a big 5′6″ with my shoes on. One time I was told to push a lady around the dance floor who was about 6′2″. She must have weighed about 200 pounds. I wasn't too crazy about the idea, but the hotel owner, Ma Holder, said, "You dance with her or you lose your job." I danced.

The big act at Young's Gap was Artie Lewis and Peggy Ames, a famous old vaudeville team. Their jokes included:

"How did you find the steak last night?"

"I picked up the potato and there it was."

And then there was this one:

"Waiter, I want to send back the steak."

"I can't take it back."

"Why not?"

"You bent it."

I got to know a lot of show business people then. One fellow I became friendly with I used to call Moishe. His real name was Merrill Miller. That was before he changed it to Robert Merrill.

ROBERT MERRILL: Young's Gap was the second hotel I worked in; I started in Schroon Manor in the Adirondacks, as a straight man to

"Blackie" Schackner kneels in front of a group of social staffers enjoying a Catskill afternoon.

"Sha-Still, the Rabbi Is Coming!" a showstopper from a Mike Hall staff production.

Red Skelton. All the performers were part of the social staff. We were put up over the social hall, which was also the theater. I got $200 a month and worked twelve weeks with free room and board. That was good money back then. More important, it was the first time I was performing. I had never been on the stage before.

I was a voice student during the Depression who dreamed of one day singing in the opera. But times were hard then. You had to go out and make a living.

One day I was on my way to a singing lesson when I saw a lineup of people in front of Steinway Hall.

"What's going on?" I asked.

"We're here for summer jobs in the Catskill Mountains," someone said.

"What kind of jobs? Waiters? Busboys?"

"No, social staff, performers."

I got on line even though I had no music with me. When I finally got in the building I saw a guy playing the piano and a bunch of people listening to different singers. Then my turn came.

"What do you want to sing?" the piano player asked me.

" 'The Donkey Serenade,' " I said.

"Where's your music?"

"I left it on the subway."

"What key?"

"Any key you want."

He played "The Donkey Serenade," and I sang it. Then one of the people listening asked me to do another song.

"Do you know 'Ol' Man River'?" I asked the piano player.

"What key?"

"Any key you want."

He played it, and I sang it. I got the job, but it turned out to be in the Adirondacks, not the Catskills.

By the next season I had an agent, and he said, "You're going to the Borscht Circuit. The money is better there." He got me a job at Young's Gap. Ma Holder ran the place like a tyrant. She booked everyone, staged all the acts. I not only sang, I did comedy, performed as straight man, danced in the finale. During the week it was suit and tie, but on weekends it was black tie. On Saturday nights I would do the big aria from *The Barber of Seville*. It always stopped the show.

Maybe because I sang opera, I always seemed to end up with the ugliest girls when we had to dance with the guests. I used to get proposals from mothers and fathers—and at other hotels, too, later on—that they would make me a star if I went out with their daughters.

The next year I worked at the Nevele. Jan Murray was the tummler there, and we bunked together. The Nevele bragged they had an opera singer, which raised them on a cultural level above the other hotels. We took off after the Saturday afternoon broadcasts of the Metropolitan Opera and did Sunday night concerts. Jan Murray would get on the microphone and explain the stories behind the arias, give the people a little background on Verdi, Puccini. The people there didn't know who the hell they were.

I remember working at a little hotel run by two partners, Lushnick and Tobachnik. One limped and was the impresario. The other was always in the kitchen making sure the portions weren't too big.

Mountain-climbing, Catskill style.

Audiences were wonderful in those little places, but sometimes they'd start to talk. You'd walk out, wait till they got quiet, then come back in. One of those places had a toilet in the theater. It wasn't so much a theater as an upholstered barn. Periodically during my act a child would scream, "Mommy, I've got to go." And you had to stop and wait until they finished.

One summer I played a bit with The Three Stooges. They used me in an act that was quite physical. I had to run on stage and tackle one of them. That night I was wearing a beautiful white dinner jacket, and the jacket got ripped. That was a catastrophe for me. But they chipped in and got me a new one.

Those summers paid for my voice lessons. My mother loved my working there. From the day I was born, she wanted me to be a singer, and she was so happy I was earning money from singing instead of working in some sweatshop like my father. At the same time, I was getting tremendous experience, developing rapport with audiences. I didn't know it at the time, but the Catskills was for me, like so many others, a marvelous training ground. We never thought of what we would become. We just went ahead and did it.

JULIE SLUTSKY: We managed to have singers on our social staffs like Robert Merrill and Regina Resnik, who sang popular songs when she was here. Jan Peerce played the fiddle in our orchestra in addition to singing.

DAVE LEVINSON: The Ritz Brothers began in the Catskills as social directors, tummlers, clowns. Their sister Gertie stayed with us at Tamarack Lodge.

They went to the Nevele one weekend during the summer of '29. They weren't even working there, but they raised such hell that Joe Slutsky threw them out and told them never to come back. Since their sister was here, they came on over to Tamarack. Then they became famous.

JACK EAGLE: I got my first job in the Catskills about 1939, as a fourteen-year-old trumpet player at the Harmony Country Club. Today it's Kutsher's Sports Camp, but at that time it was a very thriving hotel, kind of left-wing, for people who hadn't made up their minds about which way they were going—people, as they used to say in

Yiddish, "fin di linke zeyt" [from the left side]. To look at the clientele you'd never think they were socialists or interested in politics: they were a labor crowd using nonunion musicians—a bunch of fourteen-year-old kids. The waiters were nonunion too.

The entertainment staff included the chauffeur, who performed in the shows; an interpretive dancer; and Maxim Broden and Zella Zlotkin, who put on skits. There was a drummer I did comedy with. It was an education for me. I never knew I was funny before. The only entertainment was done by the staff, but on Saturday night they would bring in an outside act like a Russian accordion player. We made maybe $12 a week. And they fired us before the Jewish holidays.

ROBERT TOWERS: Around 1933–1934, while I was in law school, Murray Posner, a fraternity brother from another law school, asked me if I'd like to be director of activities at his father's hotel in the Mountains.

Here I was, a boy from the Lower East Side, who grew up in the Williamsburg section of Brooklyn, who graduated from Boys High School. I said, "Which mountains?" In geography books I learned there were the Urals, the Rockies, the Andes. Who ever heard of "the" Mountains? When your father owns a grocery store on the Lower East Side, when you go to work for an uncle at the ripe age of twelve

Taking to the water at Unity House, a cooperative resort with a left-wing slant, 1927.

walking across the Williamsburg Bridge to Rivington and Allen streets under the Second Avenue el and making egg creams at his candy store, this type of luxury you didn't know.

My idea of a summer vacation was chalking out a punchball field on the local streets, playing a game of stoop ball, stuffing a basket with newspapers and shooting baskets against the adjoining wall of a tenement house. And now here I was thrown into a thing called the Brickman Hotel in a place called South Fallsburg with no idea of what I was expected to do. I had a girl on my staff who was a blues singer, a guy who was a porch clown, and I was director of activities. The first day, just before the Fourth of July holiday, there were about sixty guests.

I said to my kids, "Look, I read somewhere about what they call an aquacade. You bring people down to a pool. You get four girls and you do rhythmic swimming. Then some guy dives off the board, then two guys have a race. And for twenty-thirty minutes, you do a shmay-dray with the people, and you keep them excited and happy."

The patriotic spirit stimulated by World War II was evident in *A Patriotic Revue*, a Mike Hall production, where dining room staff doubled as performers.

One guy said, "What will we use for lights?"

I said, "We'll bring down one of the cars and shine the headlights on the pool." And they loved it. The aquacade was a rip-roaring success.

I got the idea that people should be guided through activities: swim lessons, dance lessons, a show at night. One day a farmer came over to me and said, "You know, I get $1.50 for a horseback ride. How about becoming my agent? You get the riders, and I'll give you half a dollar a ride."

Now when your salary is $5 a week, it doesn't matter if you don't know the front end of the horse from the rear. I went around from table to table at night telling people, "You must take up horseback riding. It is a great sport, the sport of kings." I knocked on people's doors at six in the morning and got them out for a ride. I even got a horn and blew a Tallyho cry.

Now I did not know how to ride, so I wrote away to Spalding's for a book on horseback riding. It came in the mail; I studied it. At the end of six weeks, I had the sorest backside in the Catskills, but I could grip the saddle with my knees, and I knew how to lean. I earned $550 that summer. I was able to augment the salaries of the boys on my staff with riding lessons.

By the next summer we had 1,500 riders, and 1,800 the summer after that. I gave birth to the corral at Brickman's, and the hotel was launched as the first equestrian resort in the mountains. This was long before dude ranches, when riding in the East was a luxury only the rich could afford.

After I was at Brickman's for three years, I was invited to be the director of activities at Paul's Hotel in Swan Lake. Paul's was very famous in its time. It drew a crowd of schoolteachers, one of the few groups with fixed incomes. We made Paul's into a great tennis resort.

One day, Jennie Grossinger came to see me, accompanied by a man named Milton Blackstone. Billy Reed, one of their social directors, was leaving. Would I care to come and work at Grossinger's? Well, let's face it, Grossinger's was the place. The pilgrim wants to go to Mecca. Grossinger's was the apex, the place where, down the road, Meyer Weisgal, public relations director of the Jewish Agency and also of the Chaim Weizmann Institute of Science, would ask, "Bob Towers, do you think Chaim Weizmann would be happy at Grossinger's?"

TWO

THE "G"

PAUL GROSSINGER: My mother's family came to the United States around 1910 from a section of Poland that was then part of the Austrian Empire. They settled in New York City and tried to make a living in the needle trade, and then they opened a restaurant. But they were farmers and wanted to get out into the country. They thought about Connecticut but ended up in Ferndale, New York, because a very orthodox community was there already and they felt more comfortable.

In 1914, my maternal grandparents, Selig and Malke, and my parents, Harry and Jennie (who were first cousins, incidentally—I'm

How it all began: the Grossinger Kosher Farm, 1914.

100 percent Grossinger), opened a nine-room farmhouse. There were fifty acres, a broken-down old barn, a cow, a horse, a few chickens. They wanted to grow potatoes, but the soil wasn't good for crops.

So they got the idea of renting out rooms, and that's how Grossinger's began. Conditions were primitive. The only outhouse was fifty yards from the farmhouse. The Grossinger Kosher Farm of 1914 grossed $81 from nine guests, each of whom stayed a week. But the next year so many people wanted to come up that they stayed in tents scattered around the property. In 1919, the family moved a mile away to the Nichols farm. It was situated on top of a mountain, had a lake on the property, and moreover was a real hotel with indoor plumbing, electric lights, and a lobby. They renamed it Grossinger's Hotel, and with that, the whole thing was on its way.

One thing I remember about the early days is that we had our own cows, and a big activity was going to the barn to get fresh milk. I wonder how healthy that was, but people had a lot of fun doing it.

Until I was twelve years old, we lived in Room 17—my mother, father, aunt, and myself. Then my sister Elaine was born and Dad built a house for the family that was called Joy Cottage. It was a ranch-style house and sat right in the entrance to our property. We always lived on the property. After I got married, Dad built a home for me, and later he built one for Elaine.

We weren't the first hotel in the area. There was Youngsville, Stevensville, White Roe, Waldmere, Morningside, Young's Gap. But soon Grossinger's became the biggest.

Jennie was the figurehead, the image, but everybody was active in the hotel. My father was in charge of all the construction, the maintenance. Until he died in 1964, he went down to New York twice a week to buy all the fruits and vegetables at the Washington Market. He supervised the kitchens. Later I took over some of that.

Don't forget, we had 800 acres, and in my time I covered all of it. We had our own water system. We brought in whatever became popular: rowboating on the lake, swimming pools indoor and outdoor, tennis, golf—we had it all.

Through the years, the whole ambience of the place evolved. It started small, but then it grew. The architecture was Sullivan County Tudor. It got to be a glamour spot, a haven for celebrities. During the summer, it was one big family—the staff, the guests, the Grossingers.

ROBERT TOWERS: In 1926, Harry Grossinger's brother-in-law recommended a young student from Lehigh University to the family. His name was Milton Blackstone, a translation of the original Schwarzstein. Milton became acquainted with Jennie, served as a kind of tutor to Paul for a while, and then became the public relations man for the hotel.

If anyone from Grossinger's failed to mention Blackstone, it would be a sin. Because it was Milton Blackstone who made Grossinger's an international symbol of hospitality, the single best known hotel in the world, and Jennie Grossinger the first lady of the hotel business. Milton Blackstone's devotion and dedication to Grossinger's was complete. He was intuitive, brilliant, had a feel for public relations and finding second lieutenants that was second to none.

EDDIE FISHER: Milton was complicated, a man of many dimensions. He was very strange, but a man with a mission, a man who had vision. When he was twenty-three years old, Jennie said, "Let him do whatever he wants to do." He worked for Grossinger's for over forty years.

Public relations man Milton Blackstone worked for Grossinger's for over forty years. He is credited with bringing up the who's who of any given era to the hotel.

ROBERT TOWERS: In the early 1930s, a taxi driver named Moe Weissberg foiled a holdup attempt and became a kind of local hero. Milton Blackstone invited him and his wife for a two-week vacation as Jennie's guests. What publicity that gave the hotel! Grossinger's made all the newspapers.

JOEY ADAMS: In 1934, Milton Blackstone got the idea of having lightweight champ Barney Ross train at Grossinger's. Jennie went for the idea, but her mother wouldn't hear of it. "A fighter on my grounds? Never!" she said. But when Blackstone explained that Ross was an Orthodox Jew, ate strictly kosher, and didn't work on the Sabbath, she agreed.

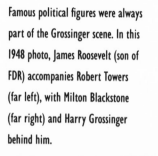

Famous political figures were always part of the Grossinger scene. In this 1948 photo, James Roosevelt (son of FDR) accompanies Robert Towers (far left), with Milton Blackstone (far right) and Harry Grossinger behind him.

ROBERT TOWERS: Barney Ross brought up Damon Runyon, Dan Parker, all the American press that covered fights. Damon Runyon got up at 6 A.M. to watch Jennie Grossinger milk the cows. He wrote about it in his column and called Grossinger's "Lindy's with trees."

MIKE STRAUSS: When it was announced that Barney Ross was going to train at Grossinger's for his title bout against Jimmy McLarnin, the

crowd at the smoke-filled Stillman's Gym in Manhattan supposedly raised their hands in alarm and cried out, "The fresh air up there will poison Barney!"

Barney Ross ignored the carnival atmosphere that developed around him and got to bed every night before ten. Almost the entire staff at Grossinger's turned out to see him fight McLarnin.

IRVING RUDD: I'm a Jewish boy from Brownsville. My dad drove a truck. You know the old line: everyone was poor but they didn't know it. I'd never heard of Grossinger's until I learned that Barney Ross was training there. All the top sportswriters filed stories with Grossinger's as the dateline. That put the place on the map.

MILTON KUTSHER: Because of Blackstone, Grossinger's got a running start on all the other hotels. At Kutsher's we tried to emulate Grossinger's, tried to follow their pattern.

I used to run a theater in Liberty. I'd meet Blackstone in Singer's Restaurant, and he would argue with me. "Why are you stopping me from getting movies in Grossinger's?" he'd ask.

"If I let the hotels have movies," I told him, "the theater would be out of business."

So every Tuesday night, Harry Grossinger would bring people to our theater. Milton and I would stand inside the lobby and discuss things of the time.

ROBERT TOWERS: Blackstone would run into Milton Berle in New York City—he was a nobody in those days: "Come up to Grossinger's for a couple of days on the house." To Buck and Bubbles, to other black entertainers: "Come on up and spend some time here." He'd meet Richard Tucker: "Come on up to the Mountains and stay at Grossinger's for a while. You'll have a great time." They came up. Alan King, Red Buttons, Eddie Cantor. They were Jennie's guests. They vacationed, they'd hang around, we'd get them to entertain.

I'd get hold of Eddie Cantor. "How about going on tonight?"

"Bob," he'd protest in that high-pitched voice, "what do you want from me?"

"Come on, Eddie, you'll do a little 'If You Knew Susie,' a little 'Ida Sweet as Apple Cider.' "

I'd say, "Ladies and Gentlemen, he innovated radio, you know 'I'd Love To Spend This Hour with You,' he fights our causes." How could he refuse? We didn't book him for entertainment, but he entertained.

PAUL GROSSINGER: These stars came for the weekend, and they'd play without pay. We called them the Good Gracious Grossinger Guests.

ROBERT TOWERS: Blackstone was responsible for changing the hotel's postal address from Ferndale, New York, to Grossinger's, New York, when Rocky Marciano trained there in the 1950s. What would any hotel owner give to have its own post office, its own zip code? You can say Hilton, you can say Ramada, but if you went into any restaurant in New York City and said Grossinger's, everyone knew what you meant.

When you made Grossinger's, anyplace else was downhill. Marty Tannenbaum, who later became chairman of Yonkers Raceway, told me how he used to start out from his home in the Bronx at dawn and arrive at Grossinger's with his banana sandwich and get into a softball

Backstage at the New York Paramount in the 1940s with Frank Sinatra (second from left). Jennie is third from left, her daughter Elaine is fifth from left. Robert Whiteman is on the far left.

game. After lunch he'd check in. All afternoon he'd go swimming at the lake, play some more softball, have dinner, breakfast the next morning. After lunch, he'd stay till the sun went down, then back to the Bronx. "Bob," he'd say, "I stayed two days at Grossinger's for $8."

ERNIE HARING: Robert Whiteman, the manager of the Paramount Theatre, was a frequent guest and would book many of his acts from those he saw at the hotel. He picked one of our bellhops, Eugene Pleshette, a very handsome man, to become manager of the Brooklyn Paramount. It was an elite job. Eugene went on to become the father of Suzanne Pleshette.

ROBERT TOWERS: In 1942, Robert Merrill was a star of the Saturday night show in the Terrace Room of Grossinger's. He was getting maybe $50 a shot. This was the same Merrill Miller a.k.a. Moishe Miller, a.k.a. Morris Miller who got out of New Utrecht High School and drove a bread truck for his uncle. Who dreamed of college?

There was a guest in the Terrace Room who sat there smoking a pipe. It was Moe Gale, who ran the Savoy Ballroom in Harlem, one of the most brilliant, independent impresarios of the era. He said to me, "Bob, I want to meet this kid."

I said, "Moe, Route 17 is strewn with the broken hearts of kids who have worked in the Mountains." You know how people expand when they're a guest at a hotel. A guy would say, "Kid, when you get to the city, call me up. I can do something for you." Then the kid would call, and the guy would say "Who? I'll meet you for a cup of coffee at Dubrow's."

I said, "Moe, don't do this to Merrill Miller."

He said, "Bob, I'll tell you what. In six months, he'll be the lead singer at Radio City Music Hall. In two years, he'll be singing at the Metropolitan Opera, the lead baritone roles."

In six weeks, he was the lead singer at Radio City. In April 1945 he won the audition for the Metropolitan Opera and became one of the world's leading baritones.

Eddie Fisher and Jennie Grossinger flanked by Milton Blackstone (left) and Rocky Marciano in 1953.

JOEY ADAMS: Milton Blackstone hired Bob Towers as social director. It was Bob's idea to attract people from different walks of life to Grossinger's. He imported such world headlines as Dr. Chaim Weizmann, Dr. Stephen Wise, and Dr. Hillel Silver. He also lured sports figures like Bill Tilden and Sam Snead. Everything was on the house for these celebrities, and champagne flowed like borscht.

ROBERT TOWERS: After Babe Didrikson Zaharias won the Women's Amateur Golf Championship in 1947, I said to my receptionist, "Babe Didrikson's in Scotland. Get her on the phone."

Receptionists are geniuses. She got through to her early in the morning their time. I said, "You've got to forgive me for waking you up, but I'm going to make it worth your while."

Babe said, "What do you want me to do?"

"Play a golf exhibition at Grossinger's next Saturday."

"Grossinger's? Never heard of it. How much?"

"$300."

"I'll be there."

The Babe came up on Rosh Hashanah week. The old New York Yankees pitcher Lefty Gomez accompanied her. Babe got out on the golf course. There were people there who did not know a putter or a driver from a plate of matzoh ball soup. They followed her around. She was a household name. She was thrilling. For her last shot, she got down on the green, took a putter, and boom!—like a pool shot—she put the ball into the hole. The crowd went wild.

Two days later: "In the pastoral bucolic beauty of Grossinger's Hotel, Babe Didrikson gave an exhibition . . ." On the AP wire the news went out to 4,000 newspapers all over America.

ARTHUR RICHMAN: I got to know Bob Towers back in 1943 over the phone. I was a copy boy in the sports department of the New York *Daily Mirror*. One day he said, "How would you like to come up to Grossinger's?"

I had heard of Grossinger's, but I knew I couldn't go there on the twelve bucks a week I was making.

"No, no," he said, "you'll be our guest."

"No. I can't. My mom said I should never accept something like that for nothing."

Golfer Alice Bauer tries to measure up to basketball star Bob (Zeke) Zawoluk on the Grossinger dance floor, 1950.

Paul Grossinger (center) with two men who made things happen at Grossinger's: Robert Towers (left) and talent booker Mort Curtis.

But he insisted, so I went up, together with two guys who were on the famous Columbia Lions football team. They were two of the biggest football players of their day: Gene Rossides, who went on to become assistant secretary of the treasury under President Nixon, and Lou Kusserow, who later went on to work for NBC as a producer.

Grossinger's at that time was as luxurious a place as I had ever been in. I was very impressed.

I knew they went in a lot for famous boxers, so I asked if they would be interested in having some baseball players come up there and they said yes. You could go on record as saying that I sure as hell was the guy who brought the baseball people up there. The first guy I brought up was the pitcher Jack Kramer—Handsome Jack, as he was known. Then as I moved up to become a sportswriter for the *Mirror*, I brought up Dick Wakefield of the Tigers and later Mickey McDermott, another pitcher, who liked it so much that he asked if he could have a job for the winter months. They gave him a job supervising athletic contests. Later on, I brought guys like Don Larsen, Tony Kubek, Dick Williams, and Saul Rogovin.

I used to give them the ground rules before we got there. "Don't ask for bacon or ham with your breakfast. Don't ask for butter with the meat. Don't smoke in the dining room on Friday night or Saturday." They all behaved. They all understood. Don Larsen protested a little, saying, "These are the strangest ground rules I ever heard of."

ROBERT TOWERS: From time to time, I would visit my mother in the Crown Heights section of Brooklyn and brag about all the famous people I brought up to Grossinger's. But she was hard to impress.

"Mama, I brought the great boxer Barney Ross to Grossinger's."

"Who is Barney Ross?" she asked. "A fighter? A 'vilder khaye' [wildman]?"

Another time, I said, "Mama, I brought the baseball star Hank Greenberg up to Grossinger's."

"A baseball player?" she said, dismissing me. "A 'shtekn zetser' [someone who hits with a club]."

Yet another time, "Mama, I brought Eddie Cantor up to Grossinger's."

Even this name did not impress her. "Eddie Cantor? An actor, a tummler, a nothing."

Finally I came to her one day. "Mama, this time I brought Chaim Weizmann up to Grossinger's. What do you say now?"

" 'Vus zug ikh yetst?' [What do I say now?] Now I know that a social director is not a bum."

Chaim Weizmann came to Grossinger's for his birthday in 1942, and Grossinger's became the telephone exchange for the world. Eleanor Roosevelt and Winston Churchill both called to congratulate him.

When the famous Rabbi Stephen Wise and his wife came five years later, there was no announcement in the newspapers, no press release was sent out. Yet there is an underground telegraph among people of similar ancestry and tribulation. Jewish farmers in Wawarsing, Woodridge, Livingston Manor, and Roscoe somehow heard Stephen Wise was going to be there. These farmers had one dark blue suit that they wore on Rosh Hashanah and Yom Kippur. They came out of the woodwork to see Rabbi Stephen Wise, the Lion of Judea.

The Wises had a marvelous weekend. On Sunday night they were driven back to their apartment on Central Park West. The chauffeur got out to open the door and was handed a large glass jar.

"Young man," Rabbi Wise said, "here is a jar of pickled herring. Mrs. Grossinger was good enough to give one for me and one for my wife."

While I was director of activities at Grossinger's during World War II, soldiers would write letters to me. I would answer each one. After a while it got to be 200, 300. We started sending packages to the soldiers—we called it Grossinger's Canteen by Mail—cigarettes, gum, sewing kits, whatever. It cost money. I got an idea.

Bill Tilden was the greatest tennis player in the world. I got him on the phone in California. "Bill," I said, "you'll stay at the Algonquin. I'll pick up the tab. You've got $250 to play a match for the Grossinger's Canteen by Mail. You'll get round-trip plane tickets."

He said, "I'll be there."

I rented the armory on 33rd Street and Park. I sent out announcements to 40,000 people from the Grossinger's mailing list. All I got back was $4,000 in the mail. I thought, what will I do with 5,000 seats and no tickets?

Then I read an item in Earl Wilson's column that Errol Flynn was at the Waldorf Towers. Errol was supposed to be, in the words of an old friend, Frank Shields, "the greatest diver, the greatest boxer, the greatest golfer, the greatest tennis player in the acting colony in Hollywood."

I went up to the Waldorf Towers. I said, "Mr. Flynn, you're gonna play tennis with Bill Tilden."

"Will Mr. Tilden play with me?"

"Look," I said, "for the amount of tickets we sold for Bill Tilden, if he doesn't play, he'll be out on the sidewalk in front of the Algonquin Hotel with no fee. He'll play."

We put an ad in the *Times* and *Tribune* that Errol Flynn was going to play a tennis match with Bill Tilden. We sold every seat in the house and turned away 2,000 people. It took thirty-eight policemen to get them off the floor. Women wanted to tear the shorts Errol was wearing that night. We auctioned off the racket he used, and Harry Grossinger bought it for $800. Flynn kept calling him Mr. Grassinger and Mr. Grossman.

IRVING COHEN: Robert Towers? I hated him. We all hated him. I was a busboy and then a waiter. He was the director of activities. He was young, his beautiful blue eyes used to pop out. He would walk through, hospitable, lovely host, everybody would call out, "Bob, Bob."

He'd get up and make announcements, and whatever he said to do, people had to do. That's the way he was. He had a way with words. Well, during the war years when we had Grossinger's Canteen by Mail, we painted herring barrels red, white, and blue. (Bob Towers created this thing here.) Then we situated them around the hotel.

Every Saturday night, Bob Towers used to make an appeal for the boys overseas. And he used to say we have these barrels around the hotel, whatever you want to throw in, throw in. The appeal he made was so heartwarming, people used to throw jewelry in there, honestly. When he made an announcement on Saturday nights, the little shop that sold cigarettes and stuff was emptied out. People bought out everything to throw in the barrels.

I say we hated him because he created the work. Who emptied the barrels? Who made the packages to send overseas? The guys in the dining room.

HARRY FIRST: I had been in a POW camp in Europe during the war. When I came back from overseas in 1945, I was in the hospital for a while and saw the Jewish chaplain there. He arranged for me to have a free week at Grossinger's—they had soldiers as their guests all during the war. I was a poor boy from Brooklyn, and it was the first time I had ever seen such affluence. The staff was friendly to servicemen like myself, invited us to staff parties, gave us free beer. The waiters didn't even want to take tips from us. I remember Elaine, Jennie's daughter, about fifteen years old at the time, big and gawky. And Milton Berle's mother, who was a permanent guest there, and she was allegedly stealing the jokes from other comics and giving them to Milton. Seven years later, I took my bride to Grossinger's for our honeymoon.

LEE FIRST: Afterward we returned year after year for Passover and weekends throughout the year. We even moved to Riverdale from Brooklyn so we could be closer to the Mountains. When our daughter was in school, her teacher had the class discuss the topic: "How does your mommy get ready for Passover?" And my daughter said, "My mommy writes out a check to Grossinger's."

LOU GOLDSTEIN: I first came up to Grossinger's in 1947 to play basketball for Long Island University against the Grossinger team. Then Paul Grossinger hired me to be a boat boy. Everyone would come down to the lake in the afternoon. The boats were free, but I figured out a way to get paid. There was a middle seat, where you row, and a back seat. If a guy was single, I took all the screws out of the center seat. That way he could remove the seat and lie down with

Lou Goldstein (center) became famous doing Simon Sez at Grossinger's, but in 1947, his first summer at the hotel, he worked as a boat boy.

the girl. It cost him a buck. If he wanted added comfort, I provided cushions from the playhouse. That was a buck and a half. I made $1,500 for the summer off those boats.

The next summer Paul invited me back to be on the athletic staff. The hotel was winterized after the war, so I stayed on. I began working around the clock. At night I was in charge of the spotlights. I'd watch the comedians and memorize what they did. During the day I took guests on hikes. We called it "An Entertaining Hike with Lou Goldstein." We walked 100 feet; I told a joke. We walked another 100 feet; I told another joke. I would get 300 people to join me on hikes.

A guy by the name of Abe Sharkey did Simon Sez. He let me jump in and kept increasing my time. I'd incorporate stories and jokes into Simon Sez and got good at it. The game is that all commands preceded by "Simon Sez" you obey. Any other command you ignore. I thought how long can you say to people "hips, shoulders, stop perspiring"? I made it into a show, not strictly a game. I'd start by saying something like "Let me check my brains someplace, and we'll start even." Or, "I don't know what I'd do without your help, but let me try."

JACKIE HORNER: I came up to Grossinger's as a dancer in 1953. After my first show, a waiter came backstage with a note on a silver tray. "Would you like to have a drink with me after the show? Lou Goldstein."

"Who's Lou Goldstein?"

"He's the guy in charge of entertainment and daytime activities."

"Tell him thanks, but I don't drink with the staff."

A little while later I came into the nightclub. As I passed the bar, a guy stuck his foot out and tripped me. I fell flat on my face. "I'm Lou Goldstein," the guy said looking down at me. "Now will you have a drink with me?"

That was the start of a stormy relationship.

In theory, Tony and Lucille Colon, the dance concessionaires, ran a strict operation. Anyone who worked for them was not supposed to date the guests or staff. But Lou threatened there would be no more complimentary dance lessons at 4 P.M. Lou was the one who drew the crowd for the free lessons, and the free lessons led to guests going for paid lessons. So Tony and Lucille broke their rule and let us date.

A famous Catskill romance: Jackie Horner and Lou Goldstein.

LOU GOLDSTEIN: The Grossinger family gave us our wedding. Paul walked me down the aisle. Before we started the march he asked me, "Is there anything I can do for you?"

"Yeah," I told him, "take my place."

But I was only kidding.

TANIA GROSSINGER: I was five years old the first time I went to the Catskills, and I remember the ride up, all the twists and turns and then seeing this giant palace on a hill that was going to be my home. I couldn't believe it.

My father was one of the Grossingers who settled in Chicago. He died in 1939 when I was two years old, and my mother Karla and I settled in California. I went to boarding school and heard children saying their daddies were in the war because of the Jews. About that time, Jennie Grossinger came west for a visit and suggested to my mother that we consider coming to live at Grossinger's. My mother spoke thirteen languages, had a Ph.D. in philosophy, and was a very elegant woman. Jennie said, "We'll make you the social director, you'll deal with the guests, and live as part of the family."

We went out that summer, but we didn't actually move there until 1945. I grew up there from 1945 to 1960. Even when I went to college, I came back to Grossinger's for all the holidays and summers. That was home.

In its time, Grossinger's was a magical place. People would write, "I'd like to bring my family up from the Fourth of July to Labor Day. We'd like to reserve Sadie the waitress and Meyer the bellhop. Please give us the same room and table that we always have."

There was a consistency in everything. Entertainers would do their signature routines. Tony Bennett played on New Year's Eve. Red Buttons would come in and do his version of "Sam, You Made the Pants Too Long." There was Buddy Hackett and his Chinese restaurant routine, Dick Shawn and "Glory, Glory Hallelujah," Joel Grey doing lots of Rumanian-Jewish songs especially on the High Holy Days. And on the Fourth of July, Lionel Hampton and his orchestra would always appear.

LIONEL HAMPTON: I began playing at Grossinger's in the 1940s. It was a thrill for me to play before such a high-class audience. Our band was very young and full of energy. We didn't know how we'd do, but with songs like "Hamp's Boogie Woogie" and "Flying Home," we had them dancing in the aisles. After that I kept bringing my band back to Grossinger's. I still go to the Mountains, and I play my heart out every time because the people there receive me with great respect.

ROBERT TOWERS: The people at Grossinger's—a lot of them were the garment center guys and their families. New York flourished from them in the '40s and '50s. They were the ones who had the box seats at Yankee Stadium, who got the best seats for the Broadway musicals for their buyers.

IRVING RUDD: With all due respect to the Concord, which saw the future, Grossinger's was the class act at that time.

I didn't get there until the late '40s. Kid Gavilan was training for a fight against Sugar Ray Robinson. I was up there as the camp

man. Barney Ross was there too, and I got to know him very well.

Phil Foster, the great comic, spent a lot of time there, and he loved the place. One time we met on the grounds, and I asked him, "I can understand 'Phil.' But where'd you get the name Foster?"

"Well, Irv, it's like this," he said, "I lived on Argyle Road in Brooklyn. What kind of a comedian would Phil Argyle sound like? So I took my name from Foster Avenue. It was only a couple of blocks away."

With so many famous characters, Grossinger's had that special ambience, but it always maintained its Jewish feeling. Shul on Friday nights was mobbed. There was no smoking from Friday sunset to Saturday sunset. You knew you were in a Jewish resort.

Lots of times you'd have goyisher newspapermen up there for the first time. Low-keyed guys, they'd sit down to eat, and there'd be this opulent spread. Their eyes would bulge—like, "How long has this been going on?" Jake Pitler, the old Brooklyn Dodgers coach, was Jewish, but he wasn't from New York. He came out of Pittsburgh, where he played for a team called Irontown, and he was rough and tough. Once a whole bunch of us were sitting around the table, finishing one of those big satisfying meals. Jake leaned back. "I tell you," he said, "you Hebes really know how to live."

Irving Jaffe, the great Olympic skater, was the Grossinger's ice guy. His assistant was Gene Brasen, a handsome, blue-eyed kid who picked old ladies off the ice. Tommy Holmes, the former Boston Braves

Pat McDermott, 1952 U.S. Olympic open skating champion (left) and Coach Irving Jaffee, 1932 Olympic gold medalist, on the ice at Grossinger's.

star, used to spend a lot of time up at the G. He had been a fine hockey player in his day. Tommy and Gene used to play one-on-one hockey in the rink at night with no lights. One night they came off the ice, huffing, puffing, laughing.

"Boys," they heard a voice, "you enjoy the private skating?" It was Harry Grossinger. He was the dollar watcher at the G.

TANIA GROSSINGER: Harry Grossinger was not a social animal. He was happy behind the scenes. When he had to put on what he called his penguin suit on New Year's Eve, it was sheer torture for him. Harry was happy to hang out with the construction workers, and he made it a point to go to Washington Market in Manhattan twice a week. Grossinger's didn't just order 500 dozen peaches. Harry Grossinger went down and sampled some before he bought. It was in the markets that I saw the respect Harry Grossinger was held in.

LOU GOLDSTEIN: Harry only came out on Saturday nights at dinnertime to greet the guests, but Jennie was there every night. She always moved around the dining room talking to people, and when she got old and sick, she sat at the entrance to welcome her guests.

Jennie was a gracious lady. She was self-educated right on the property. We had famous lecturers as guests, and they taught Jennie in private. It was like scholars in residence for her.

JERRY WEISS: I was Jennie's music appreciation teacher. I grew up in Stuttgart in an atmosphere dominated by classical music, and was an amateur violinist. We had an opera house, and the artists were constantly in and out of our home. Music, you could say, was always my hobby.

In 1938, just a few months before Kristallnacht, I came to America. I wound up at Grossinger's as a night clerk and slowly worked myself up to be entertainment director, a post I held for over thirty years.

Jennie was always wonderful to me, and it was my pleasure to teach her. We went through all the great composers. She knew little about classical music but had enormous interest, always wanted to learn, to improve herself. I still have a letter she sent me from Florida one winter during the 1940s. She writes of the pleasure she has listening to a Rachmaninoff concerto and wishes I were there to help her appreciate and understand it even more.

TANIA GROSSINGER: Jennie had all kinds of tutors, a charm tutor, people reading to her, giving her private instructions of all kinds. She took Hebrew lessons from a rabbi with some of the kids at Grossinger's. She took dance lessons from Tony and Lucille. Tony taught her, but she didn't dance much even though she knew how. She had a governess for her daughter Elaine and a wardrobe that was top of the line. But she had no airs.

ERNIE HARING: To the dining room staff, Jennie was untouchable, aloof. She was the empress. In 1941, just prior to Labor Day, the staff gave her a petition asking for better living conditions. (They were horrible. I had much better living conditions in the Army.) Jennie pleaded with us not to strike. She said that we were taking the bread

Mr. and Mrs. Harry Grossinger in the late 1930s.

Jennie Grossinger in her prime, the undisputed first lady of the hotel business, 1947.

out of her mouth, that she'd give us anything we wanted, but we should go back to work.

We went back, but never were asked back to work at Grossinger's after that summer. Ironically, before the petition, we presented a signed proclamation to Jennie stating what a wonderful person she was.

MOREY AMSTERDAM: I became good friends with Jennie after playing at Grossinger's a number of times. One summer I was in Rome and ran into her in the lobby of the Excelsior Hotel.

"Why Jennie," I said, "what are you doing here?"

"Well, I'm on a little vacation from the hotel."

"How nice. Why don't you come along with my wife and me this afternoon?"

"Why not?" Jennie said. "Where are you going?"

"You'll find out."

We met a little while later and drove about twenty minutes outside of Rome until we came to this huge building with big gates and crosses on them.

"What is this?" Jennie asked, seeming a bit flustered.

"This is Castel Gandolfo, the summer residence of Pope Pius. He's a good friend of mine," I explained. "I've known him since he was a cardinal and was in Washington."

Now Jennie seemed even more flustered. "But what am I going to say to a Pope?"

"You know, Jennie, in the prayers when they say 'Give us this day our daily bread'? Just ask him to say 'Give us this day our daily Grossinger bread.' It'll be a nice plug for you."

ROBERT TOWERS: Jennie had a repeat business that was unbelievable. In the old days, guys used to boast, "Jennie Grossinger made up my room." That would have meant she was the chambermaid for 123,000 rooms.

Jennie had magic. During the Depression, she attended a dinner in the area. Isaac Nemerson, the owner of the Nemerson Hotel, was present. He also happened to be a director of the Bank of South Fallsburg. Now a lot of people in the Catskills were dependent on the banks. They had to live on monies advanced to them to tide them over the winter so they could go into the next season. That evening,

Jennie walked over to Isaac Nemerson and spoke to him. Remember, he was her banker and probably more solvent than she was. And he turned around and said in amazement, "That's Jennie Grossinger. She recognized me!"

EDDIE FISHER: I met Jennie as soon as I came up to Grossinger's, and I knew right away she was a great lady. She treated me like a son, and I behaved like a son, and my mother didn't mind. My mother always used to say, "I live for my children." Jennie lived for her children, but she went beyond—her guests were her children. And she never stopped learning. Milton Blackstone was her tutor. He guided her like he guided me. But *she* didn't get into trouble.

How could I ever forget Grossinger's? How could I ever forget Jennie Grossinger, Milton Blackstone?

I came out of Philadelphia, where I had sung in temples, churches, schools, on the radio. I was seventeen when I auditioned as a production singer for the Copacabana in New York City. I sang for Monte Proser, a legendary Broadway figure, who was one of the partners. He wanted to put me in right away, but then he found out how old I was. You couldn't work in New York City if you were under eighteen.

So he thought about it, and he said, "Hey, I know what. How would $125 a week do you?" That was a lot of money. Three shows a night, seven nights a week—nothing. Monte asked me would I like

"What made Grossinger's was the publicity generated by its catering to well-known people." Here Governor Nelson A. Rockefeller (left) and Mrs. Rockefeller flank Jennie Grossinger, as Paul Grossinger looks on.

to go up to the Mountains. Coming from Philadelphia, that didn't mean anything to me. But I knew I was on hallowed ground when he sent me over to see Milton Blackstone at 221 West 57th Street. He said, "Don't you think you'll be lonely up there?" I didn't know what he meant. I said, "No."

So he sent me up to Grossinger's, and I was put on the staff. (I was never a waiter or busboy as some people think.) I was a singer with the band on and off for a few years. It was 1946, right after the war. I sang Gershwin's "Love Walked In"—that was a favorite then.

When I went out to sing for the first time in the Terrace Room, something happened between that audience and me. Whatever they were doing, everything stopped. And I was mesmerized by them. I knew the people out there were very rich—and there were a lot of people who were real show business, Broadway: Don Hartman, Danny Kaye, John Garfield—I can picture him with a cigarette, no tie; he was my idol. Something happened—I never knew what it was. It wasn't anything that I packaged. I just sang straight from the heart.

"She treated me like a son, and I behaved like a son," says Eddie Fisher of Jennie Grossinger. A filial kiss onstage at Grossinger's in 1965.

PAUL GROSSINGER: After Eddie Fisher's huge success, we had a lot of other boy singers. People would come up to me and say, "I've got another Eddie. Just listen to him."

Nothing happened with any of them. I could tell right away, although I never told anyone how. This is what it was: when Eddie sang, people stopped dancing. That never happened with anyone else.

EDDIE FISHER: When I came off the bandstand in the Terrace Room, I went over to Milton Blackstone and said, "Why don't you be my manager?" He said, "Eddie, I just don't have the time." When this man did something, he put time in. He had Grossinger's, his agency, Eureka Shipbuilding, a brickyard, Yonker's Ferry.

He was always in the same place in the Terrace Room having his Dewar's; he had a station, like. One night I walked off the stage and said, "Mr. Blackstone, give me one night a week." And that was it.

My discovery by Eddie Cantor was manufactured and manipulated by Blackstone. It was on September 2, 1949, the Labor Day weekend. I still have the picture: John Garfield, Jan Peerce, and Robert Merrill and Bob Whiteman were standing behind me. I was up there reading something, the center of attraction.

ROBERT TOWERS: Eddie Cantor was on a four-day vacation at Grossinger's. I said, "Eddie, there's a kid here. He sings with the angels. He's got the quaver of Jolson in his voice. It's like a singer, a chazen [cantor] pleading with the Almighty."

Cantor said, "Aw, leave me alone. What are you bothering me for?"

"Eddie, you gotta come and hear him."

He came. Eddie Fisher was next to the closing act. He sang "Any time you're feeling lonely . . ." He destroyed them.

EDDIE FISHER: It was like a setup. After I sang, everybody was cheering and applauding, and Eddie Cantor came out on the stage with me. He said, "Eddie, how would you like to go on a tour with me? We'll go to Toronto and Baltimore and Philadelphia, Washington and Chicago."

But he wasn't sure of me. "The kid sings okay," was all Eddie Cantor said, and he was a very tough man. It was Milton Blackstone who talked him into taking me on the road.

Eddie Cantor never said anything to me as we went from city to city. It wasn't until we got to Chicago that it hit him that I might be pretty good because the reaction was the same everywhere.

When I'd go on, I'd be nervous because it was Eddie Cantor, and he's not showing too much love. Then in Chicago, he said, "Don't be nervous, kid. You go out there and pee, they're going to love you after I introduce you."

Eddie called the record companies and said, "If you want Eddie Cantor, you gotta take Eddie Fisher." And I recorded in Chicago for Bluebird Records. I did a song called "My Bolero" and "Foolish Tears." For me this was such a sensation, I cried. When I got back to New York after the tour—and I really killed them everywhere—Eddie said, "How would you like me to sign you up and I'll pay you $500 a week." I said, "I have to talk to Milton Blackstone." Earlier I would have jumped. But that's how I depended on Milton. I called him, and he said, "Don't sign anything." I think he's still saying it now.

Afterwards, when I became famous, I always came back to Grossinger's. I used to bring up Joey Forman and Buddy Rich—they stayed in my room in a bed like an army cot but somehow we managed. I had to sneak them in. I didn't know how to bring them in the front way. All I had to do was ask. But it was a game, I guess.

LOU GOLDSTEIN: Eddie Fisher and I were roommates for a while—the Playhouse at Grossinger's, Room 5. We were both single and looking. We made up a signal between us. If one of us was in the room with a girl, we would wrap a towel around the outside door knob so the other guy wouldn't barge in.

Eddie liked to take a nap from 8 to 10:30 because he sang at 11 o'clock. Later each night I'd come back to the room, and there'd be a towel on the door. All I heard was his singing "You're Breaking My Heart." I had a lot of trouble getting into that room. It seemed like there was always a towel there.

EDDIE FISHER: My wedding to Debbie Reynolds in 1955 at Grossinger's was my idea. I felt it was my home, that Jennie and Milton—and even Elaine, as she was taking her mother's place—were my family. Grossinger's was something special in my life.

Later I came up here so many times when I was on my ass. But things change. When I needed a job and Jennie wasn't here and

The discovery of Eddie Fisher (right)
by Eddie Cantor in 1949 was a setup.
Milton Blackstone arranged the
whole thing.

"My wedding to Debbie Reynolds at
Grossinger's was my idea. I felt it
was my home" — Eddie Fisher.

Milton Blackstone wasn't here, I called Paul, I called him for a week—he wasn't there. Another time Elaine got on the phone and said, "You're too hot for us to handle." That wasn't a Jennie Grossinger trait. She took in anyone, and I was as much a part of the Mountains as anyone.

I didn't think I would be remembered, but time, for a change, was on my side.

JOAN WALTERS: Forty years after Eddie Fisher's "discovery," to the day, I saw him perform at Brown's Hotel. The voice was still magnificent, and they gave him a standing ovation.

Eddie sang a lot of the old hits like "Any Time," "Oh My Papa," and "Turn Back the Hands of Time." Then he did an Al Jolson medley and went out into the audience. He stopped by this woman's table as he was singing "Mammy." She looked up at him. The tears were rolling down her face. It was like his singing to her made her life.

TANIA GROSSINGER: Of all the stars and celebrities the one all the kids—and I guess the adults, too—loved the most was Jackie Robinson. I was introduced to him as the hotel's foremost Ping-Pong player.

"Okay, foremost Ping-Pong player," he said. "I challenge you to a game at four o'clock this afternoon."

A glittering Grossinger crowd in 1954. From left to right: public relations man George Bennett, Rachel Robinson, Lou Goldstein, Jackie Robinson, Julie Carson (MC and drummer with the Woody Herman band), Tony Bennett, and Ed Ashman (Grossinger's musical director).

Milton Blackstone (left) welcomes New York's Governor Thomas E. Dewey to Grossinger's in 1949.

I don't know how I got through the next three hours, wondering if he'd show up. But at four o'clock, there he was.

We volleyed, we talked, we played. I was pretty good, and I beat him. Up to then, that was the high point in my life. He was very nice about it, but I could tell that he didn't like the fact that a mere kid beat him.

IRVING RUDD: In 1954, when I was publicity director for the Brooklyn Dodgers, my wife Gertrude and I were at Grossinger's for a winter weekend with Jackie Robinson and his wife, Rachel. We went down to the winter sports area where I had spent a lot of time working the barrel-jump competition.

In those days, the barrel-jump contest that was big in Europe was popular at Grossinger's. It was like a running broad jump on skates. Twelve to fifteen barrels were lined up. You had to jump the barrels, land on your feet, and stay on your feet. I think sixteen barrels was the record. Skaters came to Grossinger's from all over the world, and the barrel-jumping got a lot of play in the newsreels. But I never played around with barrel-jumping. I liked my ice in a glass.

Now I looked around me. "Hey, Jack," I said, "let's hit the toboggan."

He gave me a withering look.

"You skate?" he asked.

"Not very well."

"C'mon," he said. "Let's go skating anyway."

I said "Okay," and we all went to the icehouse. We put skates on. The wives go to the rail to watch. Jackie goes out on the ice and proceeds to lose his balance and falls flat on his back. Geeez! The image of Walter O'Malley, the owner of the Dodgers, came into my head. I just blew my job: Jackie Robinson just fractured something, and it's all my fault. Why didn't I stop him from skating?

Then Robinson gets up and brushes himself off.

"C'mon, Irv, let's race!" He gives me that big smile.

So the two of us go like two drunks around the rink of Grossinger's. He's flopping on his knees. I'm sliding on my ass. We get up and keep going and flopping and going, and going and flopping, and he beats me by five yards.

"Let's do it again," he says.

Around we go. This time he beats me by about twenty yards.

"One more time," he says.

By now, he's really skating. He's such a natural, gifted athlete, he's skating like a guy who has been at it for weeks. It's no contest. He almost lapped the field on me.

Now there's a crowd that's gathered and they're cheering. He puts his arms around me, and he wasn't a demonstrative man.

"Irv," he says, "am I glad you were here with me this weekend. I had to beat someone before I went home."

BERNIE ROTH: Grossinger's had an ambience and a rustic flavor, beautiful countryside, etc., etc. But that's not what made Grossinger's unique. What made Grossinger's was the publicity generated by its catering to well-known people all over the world—politicians, writers, entertainers, artists—whoever was the Who's Who in an era. They made them comfortable and they publicized it. Tremendous public relations effort. You'd be there as a guest, and Nelson Rockefeller would be walking through the grounds. That was the secret: enticing renowned people from all walks of life, and ordinary guests could rub shoulders with them.

JACKIE HORNER: Sometimes we didn't even know who the honored guests were. One day a Japanese gentleman got off the bus at the bottom of the hill. He walked all the way up carrying his suitcase. He was sent to the back of the hotel to staff headquarters where Rosie Friedman, head housekeeper at the time, was busy giving out rooms. She couldn't understand him although he kept trying to explain who he was. Finally she gave him an apron, thinking he was checking in as a chef. It turned out he was a famous diplomat.

TANIA GROSSINGER: When Rocky Marciano was heavyweight champ and training at Grossinger's he lived with his family on the first floor of Pop's cottage. Mama Marciano came down from Brockton, Massachusetts, to cook for him. It wasn't that he had anything against kosher food, mind you, she just didn't like the way the chef made spaghetti.

Rocky and I became good friends. He didn't care for the fact that I was always dancing with the musicians. "Why don't you dance with me?" he'd ask. "Because you don't know how," I told him. Rocky went to Tony and Lucille and learned how to do the mambo. "Now, Tania," he said, "you don't have to dance with those musicians. You can dance with me."

LOU GOLDSTEIN: I always said Rocky Marciano was a guy with short arms and low pockets. One day he came to visit me in my room. A

Rocky Marciano (left) with Lou Goldstein. "Rocky had short arms and low pockets (as well as big muscles)" — Lou Goldstein.

Lou Goldstein interviews Rocky Marciano (holding mike) at Grossinger's, 1953 — and the guests lap it up.

bowl of fruit was on the table. He started eating the fruit. Soon it was all gone.

Then he moved to my closet. Rocky was 5′10″, and he had a sleeve length of 32.

He started looking over my shirts on the hangers.

"Rocky"—I had an idea what he was up to—"you ate all the fruit. Don't take my shirts."

"Why not, Lou? A couple of them look pretty good to me."

"Rocky, my sleeve length is 35½. Yours is 32. What are you going to do with the shirts? They won't even fit you."

"Don't worry, Lou," he said. "My mother will shorten the sleeves. They'll look tailor-made when she gets through with them."

"All right, Rocky." What else could I say? "Take my shirts."

He was a killer in the ring, a bull. But out of the ring, Rocky Marciano was a lovable, shy, perfect gentleman . . . even though he was a little frugal.

MILTON KUTSHER: Kutsher's was never the powerhouse that Grossinger's was, but for a brief time, on television back in the '50s, we were equal. Rocky Marciano trained at Grossinger's; Ezzard Charles was at Kutsher's. On CBS-TV, Edward R. Murrow, using a split screen for the first time, interviewed both. It was Charles and Kutsher's against Marciano and Grossinger's.

LOU GOLDSTEIN: In 1951, Randy Turpin from England was signed to fight Sugar Ray Robinson at the Polo Grounds. Randy came up to train at Grossinger's. We had reporters from all over the world. The headline would announce "Randy Turpin Takes a Good Workout Today Boxing Six Rounds," and below that was "Grossinger, New York," and then the story.

Ingemar Johansson was the ninth champion to train at Grossinger's when he came up in 1960. The list included Barney Ross, Lew Jenkins, Max Baer, Billy Conn, Joey Maxim, Randy Turpin, Gene Fullmer, and of course Rocky Marciano. Ingo brought his family and his live-in girlfriend along with him. One night he came over to me. "Lou, you take my girlfriend tonight. I'll take Jackie. In Sweden, that's what we do. We switch."

I never took him up on his offer, but we became good friends nevertheless. Ingo, then the world heavyweight champ, trained at Grossinger's for six weeks for his title defense against Floyd Patterson at the Polo Grounds.

EDDIE FISHER: When Rocky Marciano was training, I lived at the Grossinger airport. Rocky used it for his training quarters. That airport was Milton Blackstone's creation. He spent $250,000 to make way for an airport. That would be about $20 million today.

They called it Blackstone's Folly. But I knew that whatever he was trying to do, he had something in the back of his mind that eventually showed. He was way ahead of his time.

TANIA GROSSINGER: The man I was going to marry was set to fly in from Detroit and land at the Grossinger's airport. Jennie was writing her autobiography then, and Blackstone thought that my fiancé flying in to meet me at Grossinger's would make a wonderful episode in the book. My marriage only lasted a few months, and I came back to Grossinger's feeling lousy and whipped. Milton Blackstone came over to me in the main lobby. "How could you do it?"

"Do what?" I asked.

"Let your marriage break up so quickly. You could have at least waited for the book to come out."

BERNIE ROTH: When Jennie died in 1972, Milton Blackstone had reduced his ties if he hadn't already left. By the late '70s, the hotel started to decline.

ROBERT TOWERS: Milton Blackstone died at the age of 77. Eddie Fisher, Paul Grossinger, and I spoke at his funeral.

EDDIE FISHER: I said, "Milton Blackstone always had an idea for me: about advancement, my career, caring about other people, doing things." Even in his last years when he was in a nursing home, till the day he died, he always had an idea for me. That's what I said at the memorial service. I said, "I know someday soon, somehow, Milton Blackstone is going to send me an idea, a great idea."

Milton is buried in the Grossinger family plot in Liberty. I wrote his epitaph. It says: "A man of vision, knowledge, wisdom, imagination." I got that from reading something Einstein said—it was in *Time* magazine on the one hundredth anniversary of Einstein's birth: "Imagination is more important than knowledge." Milton had the knowledge, but also the imagination.

MILTON KUTSHER: After Jennie died, Grossinger's started to lose business. They always had religious people as guests, but they now went all out for the religious crowd because they had to get money from someplace. As the whole thing started to crumble, it was obvious to all of us. But while it was happening, you couldn't believe it. This hotel, which had been head and shoulders above everyone, this hotel which ran like a clock for so many years—all of a sudden it started to stumble and lost its way.

DAVE LEVINSON: Paul and I were very good friends. How did I feel when he told me they were having trouble at the hotel, that they were running behind? I loaned him $100,000—that's how I felt.

MILTON KUTSHER: They weren't spending the money. They had the same knotty pine lobbies that hadn't been changed in years. You know how many times we've changed our lobbies at Kutsher's? And even when you make them nice, they can't last very long. Styles change; things wear out. But when Grossinger's closed, even though we were competitors, we still felt bad.

DAVE LEVINSON: I was afraid I would have to say kaddish [mourner's prayer] for the money I loaned Paul, but he paid it back as soon as he sold the hotel.

Why did Grossinger's fall? It became impersonal.

LOU GOLDSTEIN: How did it feel to see all those old buildings go down, they asked me. I was subject to mixed emotions, I answered. It was something like watching my mother-in-law go over a cliff—in *my* Cadillac.

EDDIE FISHER: I know that somebody was trying to capitalize on the name when Grossinger's was sold. They wanted to have a lot of stars come up. But no stars came up, only I came up. I don't know why. They wanted me to blow up the playhouse. I said, "I'm not going to do that." But when I got up and there were 200 reporters there, I went along.

A woman asked, "Do you think Grossinger's will be like it was?" I said, "No. It could never be like it was. It could be better or worse. But it could never be what it was."

No other place in the world was like Grossinger's. Others have tried to copy, bring up celebrities. But Eleanor Roosevelt came to Grossinger's, Bobby Kennedy came to Grossinger's. Bobby Kennedy said, "I hope you'll be as nice to me as you were to Eddie Fisher."

PAUL GROSSINGER: My whole life and the hotel were completely mixed up, mixed in together. For all intents and purposes, I was with Grossinger's from the beginning. When we sold in 1985, my sister and I had no regrets. We had plenty of memories, and that was enough. But just the other night, I dreamed about Grossinger's for the first time since we sold it. I started thinking about what the new owners have to do to get it ready. And in my dream, nothing had changed.

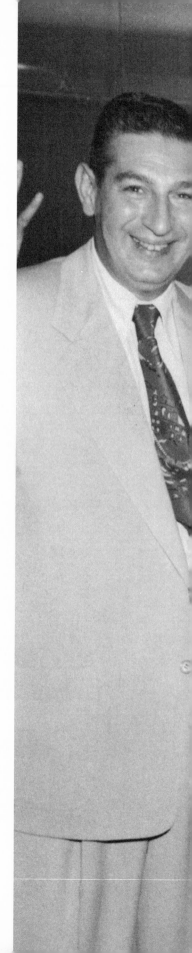

THREE

THE
10 PERCENTERS

PHIL LESHIN: In the summer of '42 I had just graduated from P.S. 43 in the Bronx. I was fourteen years old, and I went with my family to a bungalow colony called Grine Felder, which means green fields. The name was taken from a play by the Yiddish writer Peretz Hirschbein. Every once in a while we would go over and have lunch at Avon Lodge, a place two miles down the road owned by Meyer Arkin, who was also a part owner of our bungalow colony.

It was all cream-colored stucco, with green lawns, a lake, a swimming pool, even lifeguards! It seemed like a miniature Grossinger's.

Men were playing cards on bridge tables set up by the handball courts. When they lost a hand or ran out of money, they would get up and play handball. Everyone played handball then.

Crazy about the theater, just about set to start high school, I made it no secret that I was bored at the bungalow colony. Somehow I came into contact with the social director at Avon Lodge, Don Appell, who regaled me with stories about the theater. He had been John Garfield's understudy in the Group Theatre. He had done a Clifford Odets cycle, and he told me he was going to do a lot of that playwright's work at Avon Lodge using members of the social staff as his cast.

"I'll use the dance team," Don told me, "and any members of the band who have any acting ability at all. You know," he said, "I could use a young kid like you. You could play all the young parts and make up the programs."

I told my mother what was being planned for me, and she was doubtful at first. But then she must have had second thoughts about me being on her hands bored and complaining all summer. So every morning I walked to Avon Lodge, and late at night they drove me back to Grine Felder.

There I was, fourteen years old, in Meyer Arkin's office, running off the programs I had created on the mimeograph machine so that on the weekend everybody would know what was going on. I thought it was just like Broadway.

The season began. All the performances took place in the casino, which seated about 200 and was separate from the main building. The casino was on a hill overlooking the pool and lake, and you had to walk up a lot of stairs to get there. The casino was reasonably well equipped with spotlights, footlights, and overhead stage lights. There was even a rudimentary sound system.

We did Odets. We did radio plays with everyone standing on the stage around microphones. I did get to play all the young parts. Don Appell played various main characters. Lee Merrill was the bandleader and played the trumpet. The saxophone player was a young guy named Sid Caesar who also performed in certain roles.

But on Talent Night everyone really could see how talented Sid Caesar was. Impromptu, funny, insightful, he was so good that he soon became the headliner of the hotel. Avon Lodge used to import well-known comics for Friday and Saturday nights, but eventually Don had to put Sid Caesar in, the demand for him was so great.

PRECEDING PAGES

RIGHT: Al Beckman (far left) and Johnny Pransky, for many years the big Catskill talent bookers, flanking Jerry Lewis and Dean Martin, as Philly Greenwald looks on.

LEFT: Alan "Blackie" Schackner (left) and Red Buttons began in the Catskills as social staffers, but after World War II they were booked by agents into different hotels and became well-known show business personalities.

People would leave other hotels and the acts they had paid to see and would come to Avon Lodge to get a glimpse of this brilliant young comedian. It got to be so crowded that there was no place for people to even park their cars. When Sid was on stage, every seat was taken, and people would stand around on the porch that ringed the casino looking in through the windows.

Sid was already doing his airplane routine, where it actually seemed like he became an airplane. God, I thought—along with everyone else—how wonderful! Sid also did his penny gum-machine shtik and played fantastic saxophone solos. He was one hell of a musician.

Sid and I both loved classical music, and when we found this out about each other, we became friends. I had brought my phonograph up to the Mountains along with two classical records: *The Sorcerer's Apprentice* and *Finlandia*. Through those summer nights, Sid and I would sit in the bunk where all the help slept, and I would play the records over and over again. He would do amazing things with *The Sorcerer's Apprentice*, imitating the instruments and doing little bits along with the music, much like Walt Disney had done with Mickey Mouse in *Fantasia*.

After that summer at Avon Lodge,
Sid Caesar went on to become a big
star. Here he is flanked by Mary
Healy and Peter Lind Hayes. Al
Beckman is at the far left.

Late at night, after the show, we would go into the kitchen for milk, cake, cookies. But chefs are very temperamental, even in Catskill hotels. We would get only so much cake, so many cookies. I wanted more cookies. So Sid would go up to the chef, a man with some Eastern European background, and talk to him in what seemed to me a Slavic accent. It sounded real, but it was all double-talk, the same kind of stuff Sid would do later on, sounding like so many different languages. The chef would be both confused and in stitches. And all the while, Sid would back up to the cookie tray, reach behind him, and fill his hands with cookies. I'd come up from the other side, take the cookies from Sid's hands, and run like hell.

Meyer Arkin had a niece named Florence Levy, a tall, willowy, beautiful girl. Sid and Florence developed a romance. I used to see them walking hand in hand together, and there were a few times they went out on a rowboat and took me along. Oh, what that did to me. There I was with Sid Caesar, who I looked on as a much older man, a talent who was receiving the adulation of the crowd. And he was all of nineteen at the time.

That summer I learned how to dance. I still remember the tunes the band played: "I'll Never Smile Again" and "Those cool and limpid green eyes, with their soft lights. . . ." It was wartime, and as the summer went on, one by one the members of the band got drafted. Lee Merrill, the leader, was the first to go. Then the piano player. I brought in my mother, who had been a professional pianist, as a replacement.

I guess Sid Caesar must have been concerned about being drafted, but he never said anything. After that summer, he enlisted in the Coast Guard, where he did *Tars and Spars*, a show that toured every army, navy, and coast guard base. After the war, it was made into a movie. He went on to do *Make Mine Manhattan* on Broadway and became associated with Max Liebman. That led to "Your Show of Shows" and "The Sid Caesar Show." And the rest is history.

Don Appell later wrote the book for *Milk and Honey*, which ran on Broadway for a hell of a long time.

I got bitten by the entertainment bug that summer at Avon Lodge, and it led to my career as a bass player. I played in Buddy Rich's band and later became his press agent and handled other musicians.

The way life works. Forty-seven years were to pass before I linked up with Sid Caesar again. In June 1989, he began appearing in Manhattan at the Village Gate. As the Gate's press agent, I handled Sid's show, and so we met again. He is still married to Florence, the girl he met at Avon Lodge, and he is still a brilliant performer doing some of the same things I saw him do that summer of '42.

MAC ROBBINS: During World War II, there were about 400 hotels in the Mountains, but there weren't enough entertainers around. That's what killed the social staffs and brought about doubling and tripling. One hotel owner would say to another, "You use this act early in the evening, and I'll use it later."

Milton Berle brings a joyous Ceil
Beckman Jacobs onstage.

DAVE LEVINSON: For years we had social staffs at Tamarack. We had as many as eighteen people doing drama, comedy, everything. They worked day and night. Then around 1940, we decided to go into booking acts with the agents Beckman and Pransky.

JOHNNY PRANSKY: Al Beckman and I began as musicians in Swan Lake, and then we started working as agents, getting people jobs as members of social staffs. From that, we went into booking acts for single appearances. In 1940, we got hired by the Concord to supply all their entertainment. One of the first acts we booked there was the black duo Buck and Bubbles. The Concord wanted big names, and they were willing to pay for them. The other hotels followed their lead, and we supplied them all.

CEIL BECKMAN JACOBS: For a while, Al Beckman and Johnny Pransky had something like a repertory theater going in the Mountains, making a circuit of different hotels. They placed weekly entertainment at each hotel: one night a concert, the next night a variety show, the next night a play, then a guest and staff show. They called the operation Rotary Productions. Like traveling vaudeville, it moved from the Morningside to the Commodore to the Stevensville, and so on. People seemed to like it a lot, but it only lasted for a few years. Maybe it was ahead of its time.

Another thing they instituted was a midnight jamboree where acts from all over the Mountains came together at one hotel on a Saturday night. It was like a comedy fest. They came to try and outdo one another. It was always a phenomenal show.

JOHNNY PRANSKY: Once we booked an act into the Concord, a Russian guy who played the accordion and sang. His name was Sasha Leonoff. Arthur Winarick, the owner of the Concord, noticed Sasha in the lobby, took him out and showed him the place. They toured the grounds, Arthur pointed out all the facilities and where the golf course was being built. They spent a couple of hours together. That night in the Cotillion Room, Arthur Winarick sees the guy on stage playing the accordion. "My God," he said, "I thought he was a guest!"

CEIL BECKMAN JACOBS: There was a Mafia presence in the Mountains, although I doubt they were guests at the hotels. It was no secret that a lot of undercover gambling took place in the back rooms. Al knew a lot of the guys who were involved in the operation but never seemed to have any trouble with them. I remember one guy they used to call Big Farfel, a charming, handsome man who collected Napoleonic jewelry. Then there was another one, Walter Sage. Al and I were living up in the Mountains at this time, but Al went back and forth to the city frequently, and I didn't drive. Still I had no trouble getting around because Walter would call me up every day and ask, "You need a lift? You need a car?" He'd drive me wherever I had to go.

Once a few days passed without Walter calling. I ran into Big Farfel. "What happened to Walter?" I asked.

"He was eliminated," Big Farfel said.

A short time after Al and I were married, we met one of those guys. He had a scar on the left side of his face that ran all the way to his right ear.

"Listen here, Al," he said, "you gotta be very nice and take care of your wife. Also, make sure you take out a lot of insurance."

GLORIA WINARICK: My father, Irving Grossman, was a well-known leading man in the Yiddish theater who for years spent his summers as a member of the social staffs of various hotels in the Mountains. He was a singer as well as an actor and used to do the old favorites like "Mayn Yiddishe Medele" and "Shtetele Belz." I spent my summers in the Mountains with my father. There were all those beautiful hotels on Swan Lake or Kiamesha Lake like the President, the Mayfair, the Overlook, with their big verandas and lovely grounds.

When the social staffs got smaller and smaller and entertainers began working the circuit, they selected one base hotel to stay at while they traveled around entertaining at different places. My father stayed at the Concord.

On Sunday nights, all the entertainers would go into Beckman and Pransky's office in New York City to get their bookings for the week. They'd come back on Tuesday and begin their rounds.

CEIL BECKMAN JACOBS: The office was a small place at 150 West 46th Street. Hundreds of people were always coming in and out, hanging around, working, using a corner or a room, a quarter of a

desk. Sammy Cahn was there for a while. So was Neil Simon and his brother Danny.

ROBERT TOWERS: Neil's father was from the garment center. He met Al up at the Concord. "I've got these two meshugge kids, Al," he said. "I want them to be pharmacists, but they love show business. They think they can write comedy. Maybe you can take them off my hands a while and let them help you around the office."

You know the children of Abraham, Isaac, and Jacob—you can never fool them with the stomach. They know food. And you can never fool them with the ear or the eye. They have an insight into entertainment. Al said to Mr. Simon: "Bring me your sons."

There used to be benefits at Madison Square Garden called "Night of the Stars." Everybody who was anybody would appear. Al took Neil along. Neil studied the comedians, saw what they were doing. Al would bring Buddy Hackett or Alan King into the office and say, "Hey, why don't you buy a joke from this guy? Five bucks, ten bucks?"

Al got Neil a job as a social director at Tamiment in the Poconos,

Three great estimators of talent: Johnny Pransky (far left), Al Beckman (far right), and Philly Greenwald (second from right). New York City Mayor Vincent Impellitteri (center) and an aide join the trio.

about forty-five minutes away on Route 209—a Catskill kind of resort. "In two seasons there," Neil told me, "I did eight original musical comedies, sixteen shows. After that Broadway was a piece of cake, Hollywood was a rocking chair."

CEIL BECKMAN JACOBS: Neil Simon has said that the time spent in Al's office inspired him to write *The Sunshine Boys*. And in *Brighton Beach Memoirs* there's an inside tribute to my late husband. It's the scene when the girl comes home from high school all excited that she has an opportunity to audition. Her mother doesn't want her to go. She insists the girl stay home and finish her education.

"But you don't understand," the girl says, "this is for the Broadway producer Mr. Beckman."

There never was a Broadway producer Mr. Beckman. It was Neil Simon's way of publicly acknowledging Al.

Al's heart was as big as the world. While he may have made a lot of money for those years, a lot of people had the benefit of it. He loved people; he loved the Catskills. Al died suddenly of a heart attack in 1952. He was at the Concord when it happened—the scene of his greatest triumphs.

ELLIOT FINKEL: Hy Einhorn and Aaron Toper were the bookers of the small places, the bungalow colonies, the kochalayns. They gave my father, Feibish Finkel, a star of the Yiddish theater, a lot of work in the 1950s and into the mid 1960s. His name might be familiar to you because in the 1950s Jerry Lewis always ended his lip-sync act with "Feibish Finkel." I never knew why. Maybe he thought the name was funny.

Einhorn and Toper had a plastic board in their office with the names of 200 to 300 places and next to them the names of 300 or so acts, and they would juggle everything together. My father would get 70 or 80 bookings during a summer. He would re-create his so-called Yiddish acts, and the audiences always reacted well to him. They were seeing one of their own.

On Saturday nights there were shows at 8, 9:30, 10:30, midnight, and 2 A.M. My father would try to do them all. Once I was with him driving from one place to another when we got lost. He stopped off at a hotel, called Einhorn, and asked for directions to the place he was booked in.

"Where are you now?" Einhorn asked.

"I'm at Joyland Hotel," my father said.

"Okay," Einhorn said. "Play there. At least we got it covered. I'll get somebody else for the other place."

JACK SEGAL: Here's how I got into the business of booking acts in the Catskills: A friend of mine by the name of Harry Moss (the family name was Moscowitz, but they changed it to Moss) organized the first dance marathon in New York City way back in 1924. We both lived on West 111th Street, across the street from each other. One day I came out of my building and ran into Harry. It seemed something was wrong. Finally he told me that his cashier had absconded with the $1,000 prize money. In those days, that was a big deal. "Don't worry, Harry," I told him. "All your friends will raise that money for you."

"Who's got that kind of money?" he asked.

"We'll manage," I said. I called a bunch of guys together, and between the $25s and $50s, we raised $525. I had a little more than the others so I told Harry, "I'll put up the rest."

I did, and everything was all right, except I saw he was paying the other people back, and I didn't see a dollar of my money. So I went to see him.

"Gee, Jack," he said, "I'll never forget what you did for me. It kept my life straight."

"That's very nice, but I don't see any evidence that you're paying me back. You can pay it out, you know."

Just then the phone rang. It was someone from a hotel in the Mountains. They needed an entertainer for that weekend.

"How would you like to go along with one of my comedians to the Mountains this weekend?" Harry asked me. "It won't cost you anything."

"OK," I said.

He got back on the phone. "The manager of my office is coming up. I want him taken care of."

I went up by car with the comedian who was to play that night. I was treated royally. When I came back to New York City, I asked Harry, "How would you like to forget the $500 and take on a partner?"

"Sure," he said. I became his partner, and that's how I got into the business.

After a while I got married and tried doing some other things. But I always kept my hands in the agent business. At one point Harry Moss offered his business to me, but I couldn't accept it so he sold it to Charlie Rapp. Some people called Charlie "King of the Catskills." He was practically king until I came back into the business.

That was 1940. I had my own company then, Planned Entertainment Productions. But it was kind of long to write out on checks so I finally changed it to PEP Shows. I started out booking six small hotels, each of which had about 80 to 150 guests. My main act was the Jarretts, a husband-and-wife mind-reading team.

In those days with gas rationing and cars overheating, it would take seven hours to get up to the Mountains. We used to double. That meant two shows in one night, the first at 9 o'clock at the smaller hotels, the second at 10:30 at the bigger hotels. Lots of acts slept in their cars or in hotel lobbies. They weren't fed properly. I knew I had to do something about that. What I did was come up with a contract that called for my acts eating in the main dining room and getting a room equivalent to any guest. The way it worked out was that the acts ate at the first hotel they appeared at and slept at the second.

Not all the hotels wanted to go along with that. I remember the owner of the Capitol Hotel in Loch Sheldrake. He had no legs and sat in a wheelchair, and he had a habit of rubbing his hand over his face when he spoke to you.

"By me," he said, "an act eats in the kitchen."

"Not my acts," I said.

"By me, I don't give them any rooms."

"Then you don't want my acts." I walked out. Three years later he came to me begging for my acts.

But there were always problems getting rooms for the entertainers. So I innovated the idea of renting rooms for my acts. I started with Mrs. Nichols who ran a rooming house in Liberty. I guaranteed her payment for twelve rooms at $1.25 a room whether I used them or not. Then I told the hotel owners, "Pay me $2 and I'll house the act myself." I was able to hustle business on the strength of the fact that hotels did not have to house my acts. Later Charlie Rapp copied that idea from me.

The second year of PEP Shows, I went from six to nineteen hotels. Eventually I built that figure up to 121. I went from a 29-room rooming

After the war, talent bookers began supplying hotels with different entertainment each night. Here Dave Levinson of Tamarack Lodge onstage with two of the Ritz Brothers.

house to a 66-room hotel for my acts. I stayed in business from 1940 to 1970, and a lot of things happened in that time.

DAVE LEVINSON: After our first season of booking acts at Tamarack Lodge—that was the summer of 1940—I was with Harry Dinnerstein, the owner of the Stevensville Lake Hotel in Swan Lake. We were out on the lake in a rowboat, talking, one hotel man to another, comparing notes. "What did you pay for cream? What did you pay for milk?" When the conversation got around to acts, I learned he was paying less than I was. Now I was supposed to be a good friend of Beckman's and Pransky's, and it looked like they ripped me off, see? So I called Johnny Pransky. He gave me excuses and so forth, but no refund.

I heard there was a new guy in the area in those days who was trying to break into booking talent in the Mountains. His name was Charlie Rapp. In the spring of 1941, there was a meeting of the hotel owners, and I was at that meeting. I favored Charlie. The Nevele said it would stay with Beckman and Pransky. So did the Concord. But the rest of the hotel people there agreed with me, and they came with Charlie Rapp.

HOWARD RAPP: At one time, there were around fifteen agents booking acts in the Mountains, but my Uncle Charlie was the busiest of them all. He began in the business when he was a twelve-year-old kid growing up in the Bronx. His first act was a boy soprano. Hearing the kid was a big success in an assembly show at P.S. 45, Charlie sold the act to my grandfather's friend who needed entertainment for a banquet he was catering that weekend. Charlie got $10; he gave the kid $5.

Later on, my father became an amateur boxer, and Charlie would book halls for the fights and bring in entertainment for the dances that were held after the fights. Then he did a stint as the talent booker for the Astor Hotel in Manhattan, which was a big hotel in its time. From there he got recommended to places in the Mountains. There were other agents there already, but some of the hotel owners gave him a shot. He delivered for them, picked up accounts, kept on going.

What made Charlie Rapp different was that he signed up all the acts he could with package deals. Most of the guests at this time were seasonal, and some entertainers still worked at one place for the whole summer. He went after them. Instead of $75 a week, he offered them $175 a week and signed them up. Instead of staying at one place, they went to the Laurels for one week, then the Windsor, then the President, and so on. That was the beginning. The performers would say, "Hey, we're not bellhops, we're comics, we're singers, we're entertainers." In that way, he created the so-called Borscht Circuit, traveling acts booked into a circuit.

During World War II, gas was rationed, and my uncle, like all the other agents, had trouble delivering acts to the hotels. He got around the problem by hiding cans of gasoline in places off of the Old Route 17 and supplying his drivers with maps so they'd know where to find them.

ALAN "BLACKIE" SCHACKNER: In 1945 when I got out of the army and went back to working the Mountains, the social staffs were mostly gone and individual acts were working different places. Gasoline was

Alan "Blackie" Schackner (left) shortly after the end of the war with Leo the Taxi Driver. People who could deliver acts were very important at a time when gasoline was scarce.

still very hard to come by, and if you ran out of gas, you were in big trouble. It wasn't a gag when booking agents said, "We don't care how beautiful your voice is. We don't care what the hell you do. How big is your car and how many people can you take up to the Mountains?"

BOB MELVIN: During the '40s and '50s, you'd get $2 a head to drive people up to the Mountains. There was an act called the Peters Sisters, two girls of enormous size. They were assigned to this guy to take up. He always took four passengers in his car. He had a fit because there was no room for anybody else. He lost $4 on the deal and never got over it.

JOEY ADAMS: I was one of the most sought-after comics. I had a six-passenger convertible Cadillac with a big trunk in the back. I could take as many as five entertainers with me, props, costumes, you name it.

JOHNNY PRANSKY: The transportation and booking sheets were laid out at the same time. If a comic was doing two shows for us in one night we gave him his show schedule and his transportation schedule. When he finished the first show, I might have him pick up the prima donna and the dance team appearing down the road. The big trouble was getting the acts home. The act that had the car was king. If he was scheduled to pick up a magician and a piano player and he got lucky with a dame, they could be sitting all night in the lobby waiting for him to show.

ALAN "BLACKIE" SCHACKNER: The Red Apple Rest was on Old Route 17, halfway between New York City and the Mountains. It had great hot dogs. When we'd finished our shows and were heading back to New York City, we'd stop there at about 2 A.M. Every act in town was there at one time or another. It was like a fraternity. You'd recount how well you did, who bombed and who was a smash.

Zero Mostel was always there and usually doing his imitation of a percolator. Gene Barry was a mediocre song-and-dance man but learning. Jackie Gleason, who played Paul's Hotel in Swan Lake, was there.

BOB MELVIN: You would hear comics talking. Phil Foster was the daddy of situation comedy. "What Phil Foster bit are you going to use tonight?" one would ask.

"I'm going to do the one about the blind date. 'Two girls leave the guys at the table and go to the restroom . . .' "

"You can't do that!"

"Why not?"

"That's *my* trademark Phil Foster bit!"

HOWARD RAPP: Two black comedians ran into each other at the Red Apple just after the Jewish holidays.

"Where'd you play?"

"Brown's. How about you?"

"I was at the Raleigh. I went over great. The people there loved me."

"Oh yeah? What did you do?"

"Oh, the usual routine. I started off with 'Shtetele Belz,' then I did 'Bei Mer Bist du Schön,' 'Tzena-Tzena' and 'Rumania, Rumania.' They were so into it, they wouldn't let me go. So for an encore I did 'Hatikvah' and 'Yiddishe Mama.' "

"You son of a bitch," the other screamed, "you stole my act!"

BOB MELVIN: The Red Apple Rest was a place for final instruction for performers. Charlie Rapp or someone else from his office would come in. "Don't go to High Hill House. We've switched you to an upgrade, Avon Lodge."

ALAN "BLACKIE" SCHACKNER: Charlie bypassed the problem of delivering acts by having his people stay for the season at one place. We became a kind of stationary traveling troupe known as Rapp's Farm or Rapp's Paradise. First we stayed at a boardinghouse in Swan Lake, then we stayed at the President Hotel. We also had a place in White Lake, and for a while we were at the Wayside in Woodbourne. There would be nearly 100 performers staying in those places.

Once there were a couple of empty rooms, and two young secretaries checked in. They wanted to be entertained. Well, it was a show that will go down in the annals of show business. Those two girls got entertained by eighty acts who had no other show that night. And the headliners were Red Buttons and Robert Merrill.

The Farm also included Gene Marvey, the king of the club dates at that time. His big thing was singing "Eili, Eili." He would pronounce it "Chaley, Chaley," and tears would roll down his cheeks. The audience would cry too. Then he'd finish and come backstage saying, "That should hold the bastards for a while." But he was a real sweet guy.

Charlie's acts had fifty or sixty dates guaranteed. The deals worked this way. Let's say an act was getting $100 a show and doing three or four shows a weekend. Charlie would say, "Instead of you winding up with $300 a week, I'll guarantee you $750 a week, but you gotta give me ten shows." Then Charlie would try to sell the shows for $150 a week. All he had to do was sell five shows, and he made his $750 back. Then he could sell the remaining five shows at $50 and still reap a profit.

The deal was smart. Good for Charlie, good for the hotel owners, and good for the act. But sometimes it had its problems.

I never wanted to take the deal. I figured the hotel owners would know I was getting less. "Naw," Charlie said, "they all know it's the deal."

I don't know what made me do it, but one time I took the deal. Charlie booked me at the Glenmere Hotel. I had worked there before,

The Glenmere Hotel, where "Blackie" Schackner did Charlie's deal.

but the owner used to book me directly for $100 a performance. He always tried to chisel me. He'd say, "I only got sixty people tonight, Blackie. Be a nice guy, and charge me a dollar a person?"

"When you have 200 people, do you pay me a dollar a person?" I'd say, and that usually quieted him down.

This time, unbeknownst to me, Charlie had called the owner of the Glenmere.

"Who do you want for Tuesday night?" Charlie asked.

"It's Tuesday night," the owner said, "business is slow."

"I'll make a deal with you. Who do you want?"

"Who do you have?"

Charlie ran down his list.

"Blackie Schackner. I like him," the owner said, "but I can't afford him. Blackie always gets $100."

"How much do you want to pay?"

"Thirty-five dollars."

"You got him."

Charlie Rapp, who became the biggest talent booker in the Mountains, was dubbed King of the Catskills.

Charlie Rapp sent me instructions. "Tuesday night, you go to the Glenmere Hotel." Now I didn't know how much Charlie was getting for me. All I knew was I was on his deal and would get paid. Like a shmuck, I go to the Glenmere, walk into the lobby. I remember it like it was yesterday.

"You dirty son of a bitch," the owner ran up shouting at me, "you dirty son of a bitch. Me, you charge $100, and Charlie Rapp sells you to me for $35. So what is he paying you—$25?"

"Get ready to do your last show here. You'll never work for me again."

I couldn't explain. I did the show. I never worked the Glenmere again. And I never did the deal again.

HOWARD RAPP: Most acts went for Charlie's deal—98 percent of them by the early 1960s, when I began working for my uncle. In the summer of 1962, he had 175 acts signed up for 90 hotels from July 1 to Labor Day. They included blues singers, opera singers, comedians, harmonica players, accordion players, tap dancers, ballroom dancers, magicians, jugglers, bird acts, animal acts, knife throwers. There was even a blind xylophonist.

Charlie found this Filipino singing group called the Rocky Fellers. He did all their paperwork and brought them to the United States. There was a father in his fifties who lugged a big bass around, and his four sons.

The thing about this group was they could hardly speak English, but on stage no one knew the difference because they learned all the lyrics phonetically. Also they didn't read music, but they had a natural harmony. Their speciality was songs of the '50s, '60s, Elvis Presley, etc., and also Yiddish songs. Like many of the black and Italian singers who sang Yiddish lyrics phonetically, they often did a better job of it than the Jewish American acts.

The little five-year-old kid would go on his knees ringside to a woman and grab her hand. "My darling, I need you to call my own," he'd sing in a high-pitched voice (and you know how Elvis sang that in his deep voice), and then he'd go back and sing the harmony. Later my uncle got them a record contract, and they had a 1963 hit, "Killer Joe."

MOREY AMSTERDAM: I got booked by the Rapp Organization during the 1950s. I was from San Francisco and had never heard of the Borscht Circuit. But after Charlie got me weekend dates at the Concord, Grossinger's, and other hotels in the Mountains, I realized what I missed by not having been in vaudeville and on the social staffs in the Catskills. The audiences there were great, they laughed at all the right places. And what did I do? What I've gone on to do for over fifty years in show business—I just got up and talked.

HOWARD RAPP: My Uncle Charlie had an uncanny way of talking to performers, hearing about what kind of entertainment they did, and then just booking them. And nine out of ten times he was correct.

"How can you give these people jobs without seeing them perform?" I once asked him.

"Listen," my uncle said. "When you're in the business a certain amount of time, you'll know. You'll get a feeling."

"Boy," I told him, "I can't wait to get that feeling."

As a teenager, spending time in my uncle's office, a place where the phone was always ringing off the hook, where there were all these charts, calendars, and lists, entertainers and managers calling and dropping in, I started to get the feeling. Big-timers, newcomers, unknowns—you name it, my Uncle Charlie dealt with all of them. He was not only a booker, he was travel agent, missing persons bureau, psychologist, nursemaid. He once had this comedian who was finicky about the crowds he played before. He was booked into the Nemerson. "I don't like the crowd there," he complained. Then he was booked into the Pines. "I don't like the crowd." In a very patient voice my uncle told the comedian, "I'm going to get Polaroids taken of the different crowds. You look at them and figure out which crowd you want to work. Then you get back to me."

Much of the business was done on the phone. I would hear these conversations: The phone would ring. My uncle answers, listens. "Sidney," he says, "I gotta get a list together. Give me a chance, give me five minutes. I have to call Bernie. Maybe I'll work a double."

Or: "Listen, doll, if you hear a guy singing 'Ol' Man River,' you certainly don't need to hear him singing 'Ochi Chorniye' . . . No? Okay. I'll get you a swell harmonica player. You know Blackie Schackner?

"You need a comedian? I've got the perfect guy for you. Great. Especially with a Catskill crowd. His price is going up next season. The kid played Laurel in the Pines a half dozen times already. He played the Nevele. A very clever guy, he's coming on. Mal Lawrence. And you know, one comic is worth five hundred baritones."

NORM CROSBY: Charlie Rapp thought that singers and dancers were wonderful, but his pets were always the comics. His philosophy was, if a fight broke out backstage, if there was a flood, a fire—forget everything and protect the comic. In his view, they were the most important part of the business. People came up to the Mountains to laugh.

HOWARD RAPP: Uncle Charlie used to say his biggest problem was not placing talent, but seeing that it got there and that the act knew who it was entertaining. Once he sent Fat Jack Leonard to a hotel in the Mountains. Fat Jack walked out before an audience where most of the men were wearing yarmulkes. His opening line: "Welcome, Legionnaires!"

NORM CROSBY: The first full season that Charlie Rapp booked me, I did about five or six shows a week. He had me crazy going from one to the other, early shows, late shows, late-late shows, encores.

Once I came rushing in late to a place. The guests were sitting around kind of casual in the dining room. A three-piece band was up on a little stage. They were high school kids. I went over and said, "Listen, I don't have any music. Just play me on, and when I finish, play me off. Just introduce me by saying, 'Here's a very funny guy: Norm Crosby.' "

Many acts stayed over after the show to take advantage of hotel facilities. Here Buddy Hackett tees off at Tamarack.

They played a little bit of a fanfare. I got introduced. Everybody paid attention. I did my act, doing then what I still do now: mixed-up words, satire, commentary on what is current, ad libs. The audience laughed and applauded. The little band played me off, and I said to the kids, "That was great. Thank you very much."

Then a little fat man who seemed to be in charge came over to me. I'll never forget him. Under his tuxedo, he had on a T-shirt. I never saw that before or since.

"You were terrific," he said.

"Thank you very much. I loved working before this audience. By the way, Mr. Rapp asked me to say hello to Jack Fink. Is he around? I'd like to meet him."

"I don't know."

"Jack Fink. Charlie Rapp told me to be sure to say hello to him."

"I don't know no Jack Fink. What does he do?"

"He's supposed to be the manager of this hotel."

"No, I'm the manager."

"Don't you know a Jack Fink?"

"Oh," the guy suddenly realized, "you're talking about *that* Jack Fink? He's the manager of the hotel across the road."

ROBERT KOLE: You could write a whole book filled with Charlie Rapp stories. Myron Cohen told me what I think is the ultimate Charlie Rapp story. Here's how I remember it.

"Driving up on Old Route 17 through New Jersey, I was in a car with Charlie Rapp, Phil Silvers, and Red Buttons. I was driving, and Charlie sat next to me. Phil and Red were in the back. It was a hot day, and the windows were open.

"On his lap, Charlie had a big, thick pad that he kept with him at all times. The names of hotels were listed in alphabetical order on the left side of each page, with who was appearing where on the right side. We were going through a town, and I stopped at a red light. A big truck pulled up alongside of us on the right. The driver looked down at Charlie Rapp.

" 'Hey bud,' he said, 'where's Allendale?'

"Charlie went to his pad, flipped a couple of pages, and looked up.

" 'Alan Dale? Kutsher's tonight, doubling at the Raleigh and the President Saturday night.'

"You had to know Charlie Rapp,
because he *was* the Mountains" —
Billy Eckstine. Here is Charlie with
Cab Calloway.

"When I heard that," Myron added, "I almost drove the car off the road."

BILLY ECKSTINE: You had to know Charlie Rapp, because he was the Mountains. Charlie could tell stories that could make a Broadway play. Things that actually happened dealing with those hotels.

NORM CROSBY: One of Charlie's favorites was about a belly dancer who he booked at a place called Mandelbaum's Mystic Manor. She showed up late one afternoon, getting set to work that night for one of Charlie's "pain in the ass customers," guys who complain about everything. Mr. Mandelbaum was the biggest pain of all.

The girl walked into the lobby, and Mandelbaum reached for the phone.

"Mr. Rapp," he started out, "the girl you sent me just got here. One look at her made me feel very sick."

"What's the problem, Mandlebaum?"

"The hair, the hair, it's all in rollers. She's wearing a baggy raincoat and shmutzik [filthy] sneakers."

"Is that all?" Charlie said. "Relax. She'll let her hair down, put on some makeup, get dolled up. She'll look terrific. You'll see."

Later that evening, Charlie called back to see how things were going. "So Mandelbaum, did she come in for dinner? How did she look?"

"Mr. Rapp, she looks much better now."

"Good. I told you."

"It's good, but Mr. Rapp, I'm still worried about her."

"Why are you worried? What's the matter?"

"I haven't seen her costume, I don't know how she looks in it. I don't know if she knows what she has to do."

"Mandelbaum, she'll look great, and she'll do great. Don't be such a worrier. I'll call you tomorrow."

The next morning Charlie called. "Well, how did she do?"

"Let me tell you how she did, Mr. Rapp. The girl came out with a nice costume on. She looked good in it. Everything fit. She put those thimbles on her fingers, and she snapped and snapped. To tell the truth, she was terrific."

"So it sounds like things went well."

"Let me finish."

"So finish."

"She danced around a pillow. She was wonderful. She made all these moves. She looked very good. Then she picked a guest from the audience, got him on stage, and had him sit on the pillow while she snapped and shook and danced around him. She was marvelous."

"So good, Mandelbaum."

"Good? Great, Mr. Rapp! But I gotta tell you something."

"Tell me."

"She doesn't know how to pick people from the audience. The guy she put on the pillow—he was terrible."

HOWARD RAPP: My Uncle Charlie would go through a carton of cigarettes a week. When he'd get excited, he'd put one in his mouth, unlit. He didn't smoke. People who didn't know him were always offering him a light.

Aside from his business, my Uncle Charlie loved to play poker. He's actually in the *Guinness Book of Records* for pulling two royal flushes in a row at the Friars Club. Also he loved to dance, and almost to the end of his life (he died at the age of seventy-two), he was taking girls to discos.

Charlie married late in life and had no children. But he was very good to his nieces and nephews. He kept the family working, took care of everyone. There were three things that he did for all of us: he paid for our college educations—those of us who wanted it. He gave us all jobs. And, most important, he paid for everyone's nose job. Charlie's wife was a French woman named Jacqueline Petite who had been a dancer and, at one time, a knife thrower. Every time she wanted to get a nose job, she'd send one of Charlie's many nieces or nephews to the plastic surgeon first to see how it came out. When I was about to have my nose fixed, she picked out a doctor for me. "He's good," she said. "He did all the chorus line girls at the Latin Quarter."

Charlie gave Jackie Mason's contract to my cousin Bob Chartoff as a wedding present. That was when Jackie was just a hot young comic waiting to go to the next step. But that gift started Bob Chartoff off in the management field. He later signed up other talent, then met Irwin Winkler, and together they went into movie production: the *Rocky* films, *Raging Bull, The Right Stuff,* etc.

As for me, I remained at 1650 Broadway, working with my uncle, learning the trade. In 1958, a young guy named Arnold Graham took a desk in my uncle's office, bought performers from him. He developed

Howard Rapp, at work.

a friendship with my uncle and myself, and in 1970 became partners with us. When Charlie died in 1974, Arnold and I became equal partners in Charles Rapp Enterprises. But by that time, I had close to two decades of experience in booking and managing talent in the Catskills. I went back to the early '60s, beginning with the summer my uncle set me up as the thirteen-year-old proprietor of the Willow Lane Hotel.

The Willow Lane was a fifty-room hotel off Fraser Road in Monticello, another one of the small places that my uncle, over the years, leased to house entertainers that he booked in the Mountains. An old couple named Stein leased it to him from the Fourth of July to Labor Day, and he put me in charge to see everyone had a room and to keep track of who was where.

It was just three white frame buildings, two stories high, set in a pine grove way back off the road. Entertainers who got stuck, or didn't want to go home between jobs, or just wanted a comfortable place to stay, had rooms there. The singers would hang out around the piano, vocalizing and working up new arrangements. The comedians would be horsing around, trying out their shtik on one another. The dancers and acrobats would be out on the lawn, doing reps and practicing new moves, or else they'd be exercising in the pool. There were lots of dance acts: Alfred and Lenore, Norton and Patricia, the Albees, Juan Carlos Cortez and his team of Latin dancers, who would get up on the table to rehearse. There were also many family acts. The most unforgettable were the Coronados. They were a singing group from New Mexico, Navaho Indians: a mother, father, children, and an uncle.

BOB MELVIN: Nobody got much sleep at the Willow Lane. The nickelodeon was loud, the acts who doubled came in late, and they wanted everybody to know so they slammed a lot of doors. It was a million laughs.

VIC ARNELL: Back in the old days, I used to go to the Willow Lane just to hang out. You didn't want to talk to civilians. When you were finished performing, you wanted to talk to show people. At 4:30 in the morning, there'd be fifty acts playing cards, having dinner. It was family.

WILLOW LANE HOTEL and CHILDREN'S CAMP
Monticello, Sull. Co., N.Y.
Phone Monticello 1500-1501

The fifty-room Willow Lane, off Fraser Road in Monticello, was one of the places Charlie Rapp leased to house entertainers.

BILLY ECKSTINE: I don't believe I slept at the Willow Lane much. It was where Charlie put supporting acts mainly. But they did have some good card games going on, and I joined in more than a few of those.

HOWARD RAPP: Gin, poker, pinochle—there were always card games. The entertainers would come back from their shows, drink beer, play cards, and talk until five in the morning about how they went over.

Norm Crosby was breaking in around that time. He had the room right across the hall from me, and we became very friendly.

One night, I had a terrible cold. I was sneezing all over the place but more than holding my own in a big poker game when Norm suddenly came in.

"What are you doing to this kid?" he shouted to the guys I was playing with. "Can't you see he's sick?" He grabbed me by the ear and pulled me up off my chair. "Let's go!" he said.

"Wait a minute," the guys yelled, "he's got all the money."

Ignoring them, Norm dragged me up to his room. He took out a bottle of Southern Comfort and a shot glass. I had never seen him drink. I don't think he drinks to this day. He must have gotten the bottle from some grateful hotel owner or bartender.

He poured out a full shot. "Gulp this down," he said. I drank. And then another. I drank. He must have kept the stuff around for medicinal purposes, I thought, because it sure tasted just like medicine.

Then he took me into my room. "Now go to sleep. That's the only way you'll get rid of that cold."

I slept. When I woke up, it was the middle of the next day. I got out of bed and went to open the door, but it wouldn't open. Later I found out that Norm had pulled an iron hanger through the hasp to prevent me from getting out.

There was no one around. I knew even if Norm was in his room, he wouldn't hear me shouting because back then, even with his hearing aid on, you had to talk right at him.

I figured my only way out was to get to the roof of the porch that ran around the building. So I pushed the screen out of the window. That took some time. I was careful not to break it. There was no air conditioning, and I had the rest of the summer to sleep in that room. I finally got the screen out, climbed out, jumped down, and was free. It was just like an escape scene in a movie, I thought. It wasn't until much later that I realized my cold was all gone.

ROBERT KOLE: The first summer I worked in the Mountains was in 1962, and I stayed at the Willow Lane. I had been in seven Broadway shows, and we Broadway performers looked down on people who worked the Catskills. We didn't associate with that end of the business. But I fell in love with it all, and I've been working the Mountains ever since.

LINDA HOPKINS: Sometimes the hotels we played in had rooms for us and asked us to stay over, but we only wanted to go back to the Willow Lane. The people there and the entertainers were family. Leslie Uggams would stay up there with her mom. She was just a little girl then, and she was like my baby.

There used to be a pinball machine that I was always playing. I put so much money into it that they finally fixed it so I could play without paying. And, as I think back on it, living out of the Willow Lane and entertaining in the hotels was like getting paid for playing.

HOWARD RAPP: On Saturday mornings, my uncle and his home staff would come up to the Willow Lane for the weekend. He had a little office there he would work out of.

My Aunt Bessie, who was Charlie's sister, was the bookkeeper, and she'd make out checks for performers on a weekly basis. One Saturday, a dance team named Slip and Slide came in to get their checks.

As a girl, Leslie Uggams stayed at the Willow Lane with her mother. She went on to perform regularly at the Concord.

"Where'd you work this week?" Bessie asked.

"We didn't."

"How come?"

"No one told us where to go."

My Aunt Bessie didn't care. She was busy, and they had a contract. That was it. She gave them their checks. This went on for a few weeks.

My uncle could relax even under a lot of pressure. He'd stop what he was doing, go out and take a little walk. One Saturday up at the

Willow Lane, he was doing just that when he overheard two guys who were sitting in the sun out on the lawn.

"That Mr. Rapp is a wonderful man. His sister is a wonderful lady," one said.

"We've got some great deal here," the other said.

"Who are you guys?" my Uncle Charlie asked.

"We're the dance team Slip and Slide."

"You like it so much around here?"

"Oh yeah, that Mr. Rapp is terrific. He pays every week. His sister is so nice with a check. We're having such a good time up here."

"How many shows have you done so far?"

"What shows? Every week we get paid. Nobody tells us to work. We eat and have fun, and go and get paid. We're having a vacation."

Charlie took a deep breath. "Do you guys know who I am?"

"No, sir."

"I'm Charlie Rapp," he shouted, "and you sons of bitches are making up every show you owe me next week!"

On Saturday nights, someone would drive over to the Dodge Inn and bring back steak dinners for all of us. My uncle would be busy in his office till about 2 A.M. Then we'd all go over to the Laurels for the last late show in the Mountains. He always had thirty ringside seats reserved.

BILLY ECKSTINE: After everyone did their Saturday night show, they'd all meet over at the Laurels. And every performer up there was in the audience. And they'd be getting up, and it was like the show would run forever. Saturday night, Sunday morning we all did the Laurels. I'd go see the shows, and sometimes I'd perform spontaneously without even having my music.

ROBERT KOLE: The Laurels Country Club was on Sackett Lake, a real lake, which made it special. It was one of the great places in the Mountains. The owner, Charles Novak, catered to a young, swinging crowd, and probably more liquor was consumed and more babies conceived in that hotel than anywhere else in the Mountains.

I still remember one of the late late shows I did there. Alfred and Lenore opened. Then I sang my medley of show tunes, mostly from *West Side Story* and *My Fair Lady*, which were very popular then. Norton and Patricia followed me as the third act. And then Dick Shawn went on and did not walk off that stage until 5:45 in the morning. And nobody left.

HOWARD RAPP: All the entertainers, big-time, small-time, got up and ad-libbed at those shows. They weren't entertaining the people; they were entertaining each other.

We'd be in that nightclub till the sky got light. Of course, I wouldn't last all that time. A security guard would bring me out to a car, where I would sleep. After the last act they'd wake me up, and we'd all go into the coffee shop. The hotel would pick up the tab in the nightclub, and my Uncle Charlie would pick up the tab in the coffee shop.

I did pickups of my own from the Willow Lane. Part of my job was making collections from hotels and bungalow colonies. I was too young to drive, so Mendel of Fallsburg, the most famous taxi driver of all time up there, would take me around. When entertainers appeared in two places the same evening Mendel was the one they counted on to take them or direct them from place to place.

In his old brown station wagon, Mendel would drive down all the back roads and lanes. At the time, I thought he was an old man. He wore a cap with a lid like the old-time cab drivers. I can still remember sitting next to him, hearing him say, "This is the road to the Stevensville. If you go this way, you'll get to the Pines." Mendel could find roads that would cut miles off a trip. Soon I knew every road, every back way all over the Mountains. It got so I was a walking road map. The acts would ask me, "Can we double the Windsor and the Lake House?" "Can we triple Kutsher's, Pullman's Bungalows, and the Nemerson?" There I was, a kid of thirteen, and these adults were asking me.

Today, I often think of Mendel as I crisscross the Mountains, going from one place to another in record time. He taught me well. One day on the way to Kutsher's, I drove off Fraser Road to take a look at the Willow Lane. It's part of Kutsher's property now. Like so many of the older small hotels, one of its buildings burned down. The others are abandoned, hidden behind overgrown grass. Windowpanes are missing, doors are off the hinges. I looked around, and boy, it was something. I remembered so well how it used to be—all the excitement, all the fun, all the crazy things that went on there so many years ago when I was a teenage proprietor of a Catskill hotel.

FOUR

THE ERA

ARTHUR SHULMAN: It will never be duplicated. Unless you lived through it, you can never quite know what it was like. It was an atmosphere, a time, an era.

BOB LIPMAN: The 1950s and '60s were perhaps the heyday of the small hotels and bungalow colonies. Some hotels were so small they only had about thirty rooms. There was a so-called solicitor, a guy or girl or couple with a following who would get a commission on the guests they brought in. The solicitor would make telephone calls or advertise by direct mail. "Come to the Carmel Hotel for the summer.

Joel and Shirley Baum"—the solicitors—"will be your hosts." This was supposed to be an inducement to stay at a particular place. And strangely enough, it was.

The Carmel Hotel in Loch Sheldrake was typical. Capacity: 200. Run by the Jacobs family, the Carmel catered to a family crowd, had a swimming pool, small lake, playground for children, one softball field, one tennis court, one handball court.

MARVIN SCOTT: Down the road from the Raleigh on the way to South Fallsburg was a signpost at the crossroads with about twenty or thirty arrows pointing to different hotels. The signs were so crowded together you really had to study them to find the hotel you were looking for.

ELLIOT FINKEL: Growing up in the '50s, I could name at least 200 hotels in the Mountains the way kids could name baseball players and batting averages. The Village of South Fallsburg had forty hotels with little lobbies, tiny dining rooms, no indoor pools.

VIC ARNELL: There had to be at least 500 hotels and 500 bungalow colonies in the mid '50s when I first came up to the Catskills from the Brownsville section of Brooklyn. It was so vibrant I thought it was the most exciting place in the entire world.

MARVIN SCOTT: Going to these places, you got away from the city streets, you were in the country, the mountains. It was economical, and the people recognized it. My father was a very hardworking blue-collar worker, but he was able to take the family up to the country for the summer. You'd think this is going to be a lot of dollars, but it wasn't, and it wasn't even that far.

JOSEPH "PICKLES" MERGLIANO: During that time, a lot of the people would come up by hack. I worked for Goldy's Limousine Service for many years, driving a ten-passenger stretch Buick. We charged $10 to $12 one way (now it's $35 or $40). Back then the train was cheaper—just $2.20, or two cents a mile from Weehawken.

Until they built the Quickway, we'd have to go on Old Route 17 through Chester, Goshen, Middletown, and all the back roads. You couldn't speed then. There were only two-lane highways with buses and trucks. Even in Jersey it was a two-lane highway into the 1940s and 1950s. Going through Middletown was a bottleneck with traffic and winding streets.

When you made the pickups there were always the arguments about who was going to be taken first. I always started in Brooklyn and worked my way up. When I drove them home, the last ones picked up were always the first ones dropped off. The biggest problem driving was taking them people home. All the hotels checked out at the same time, 2:30 in the afternoon, and the roads were all jammed up at that time of day.

In those days you had to give people a break, even though the mothers always brought food along bagged up to keep the kids happy. I would make one stop, usually at the Red Apple Rest. Everybody stopped. I remember the lines to get into the bathrooms, the over-heated cars, and the buses that stunk up the place and made it tough to even find a parking place.

ELLIOT FINKEL: There was something about the atmosphere at the Red Apple Rest that made everyone want to tell stories. A guy who sold stuff off a pushcart on the Lower East Side would suddenly become a "dry goods salesman." A presser in a factory would become a "clothing manufacturer." Since the Thruway came in, the Red Apple has been bypassed, but in its time it was a wonderful hangout.

ELAINE MARKSON: For three summers I worked as a counselor in the Mountains. I got up there and came back home by hack with a stop along the way at the Red Apple Rest. Getting up there was like the Buddy Hackett routine. The limo picked us up at 9:30 in the morning. We went to the Bronx, back to Brooklyn, across the bridge into Manhattan, picked up somebody else in Queens. Three o'clock in the afternoon, we'd still be wandering around.

Somebody would holler, "Open the window, it's too hot in here!"

Someone else would yell, "Shut the window, it's blowing too much!"

And someone else: "Leave the window open. I have to vomit." That usually settled the argument.

BILLY FEIGENBAUM: In 1961, I was working for an animation studio, but on the summer weekends, I was always shlepping people up to the Catskills. My father had a half-assed limousine service, and I drove one of his extra cars: a black '59 Checker Superba, the same thing that they made for the big old taxis—strong as an ox but slow as molasses.

I picked people up in various parts of Brooklyn on Saturday mornings, starting very early, five or six A.M. A friend of mine came along and helped me out as a favor.

We'd fit three people in the front, two in the jump seats, and four more in the back because it was pretty wide. People who got picked up last were always pissed off because they had to sit in the jump seats, which weren't too comfortable.

The ones going to bungalow colonies usually stayed for a month or so. They'd take everything—luggage, food, dishes, pots and pans, sheets and pillow cases, even ironing boards. It was like they were going to Europe. We'd get the stuff into the car any way we could—hanging out of the trunk, tied on to the roof rack with ropes. It took hours to get everything strapped in and get ready to go.

The tension would mount after all the passengers were in the car. They didn't know each other, and they very rarely got along. The Checker wasn't air conditioned. It was always hot and sweaty with all those people, and if we got stuck in traffic, ugh!

Wurtsboro Mountain was always a pain in the ass. We were always so loaded down with crap that the Checker couldn't get over five miles an hour. Then, about the time we cleared the hill, the big arguments would start about who was going to be dropped off first. They all wanted to be first, but I had specific instructions from my father, and I followed them to the letter. A couple of times I'd go past someone's destination and have to drive all the way back to drop them. They were pissed.

I still remember two single women in their forties. They asked me what I did, and I told them I was a commercial artist but that sometimes I also worked at the Concord.

"What do you do there?" one of them asked.

"I don't know whether I should tell you this or not."

"Oh please, tell."

"OK. I'm a stud."

That got them all excited. "Ohhhh. We'd like to make a date with you. When can we see you?"

They were out for men or boys or whatever they could get. They didn't get me, but I always wondered what it would have been like.

I also remember this guy about seventy years old said he was going up looking for "young stuff," women in their fifties. Flowery tie, beige shirt, shiny suit. He said he wore it going up so it wouldn't get wrinkled in the suitcase.

I sure was wrinkled—that Checker was a bitch. It took a minimum of three hours just to drive there, and then there was all the time spent picking them up, packing in all their stuff, playing with the ropes, dropping them all off. It got so that I could make the ride in my sleep. Sometimes I thought that's what I was doing.

After that summer, I told my father I didn't want to give up my weekends that way anymore. He understood.

ELAINE MARKSON: When I think about those times, it makes me smile. How much simpler things seemed then. You went on vacations with your families. That was the way the lifestyle worked.

MICHAEL TRAGER: From the time I was seven until I was eleven, I went with my grandparents to the Fallsview Hotel for the week of the Christmas holiday. The three of us used to drive up, and the

Interior elegance during the "era": the lobby at Brown's Hotel in the 1950s.

rounded shapes of the mountains would remind me of whales. The owner would come out to greet and hug my grandparents, and they would laugh together. Years later, I learned they were all longtime friends.

I remember the snowmobiles in different colors on the snow-covered lake, the indoor heated swimming pool, the games of Ping-Pong, shuffleboard, and billiards. It seems now those times were the best of my childhood, although there were two things that I never got to do. One was see the Monster at the Concord. I didn't find out it was the name of a golf course until I was grown-up. The other was eat in the main dining room, which seemed so big and exciting with all the glasses clinking and the shiny silverware laid out on the tables. But, being a kid, I had to eat in the children's dining room.

MARNIE BERNSTEIN: In 1955, we went to the Catskills for our annual two-week vacation—my mother, my little sister, and me—and this summer we took along a cousin, a girl my own age. We were headed to Robin Hood Inn in Ellenville, a small family-run establishment typical of hundreds of hotels that existed in Sullivan and Ulster counties in those days. As always, my father had to work, but he would come up for the weekend during our stay.

I still, after all these years, get a pang when I think of those farewells. Even now I can see him standing on the corner in front of our apartment building, waving as the hack pulled away. As I strained to keep him in sight through the back window, I'd see him turn and walk back toward the building just before the hack turned the corner and we were truly on our way.

But moments later, my thoughts were on the country and on the possibilities of two weeks away from Brooklyn and the chance to meet new, and hopefully older, boys. The trip was tedious and long because the hack made several other pickups, one in Borough Park, another in Williamsburg, and then over the Williamsburg Bridge to a third pickup on the Lower East Side. I remember there was a woman who was terribly amused when my little sister asked how old I was going to be in the country, and I said sixteen. "You won't be making yourself older much longer," she said.

This was to be our third visit to Robin Hood Inn and, although I had no way of knowing it then, the last time I would ever go to the country with my family. That's what we called it, "the country" as

opposed to the Bensonhurst section of Brooklyn where we lived, which to me was an area of unrelenting dreariness. I longed for the Mountains.

And there they were—a backdrop to Robin Hood Inn: three small white frame buildings sitting on a little hill in the Ellenville valley, overlooking the road. Our room was in the smallest building; it was both square and spare and had two iron double beds, a simple dresser, and a washstand. The bathroom was down the hall.

What did one do at Robin Hood Inn? Play canasta on the wide wood-planked front porch of the main building, pitch horseshoes, lounge in Adirondack chairs on the deep lawn that sloped down to the road, play handball against a whitewashed wooden wall that said:

ROBIN HOOD INN

MEYERSON AND ROGOW FAMILY

HOTEL AND DAY CAMP.

My sister attended a rather rudimentary day camp run by a beautiful and buxom blond named Blanche who read *Seventeen* and *Mademoiselle* and knew the names of all the fashion models. She was, we heard, a "refugee" and had those mysterious blue numbers tattooed on her arm.

And then there was the "Beautiful Modern Pool," the crowning glory of Robin Hood Inn and the subject, in artist's rendering, of the

ROBIN HOOD INN, Ellenville, N. Y. Beautiful Modern Pool.

E 8751

An artist's rendering of the "beautiful modern pool" at Robin Hood Inn in Ellenville, around 1955.

At small hotels and bungalow colonies, the swimming pool was often the most glamorous spot and the favored setting for photographs.

hotel's postal card. It was a square of aquamarine with a concrete deck on two sides and a white chain link fence around it. Aside from the casino, the swimming pool was the most glamorous spot on the property.

In reality, the casino was no more than a large finished basement beneath the main building. But like the song they played that summer, "Oh! What It Seemed to Be," I thought it was glittering and sophisticated with its blond wood-paneled walls and gleaming dance floor. The access was through an exterior stairway railed with wrought iron. And poised at the top of the stairs in the dusk of a mountain evening, wearing a dress of some gossamer fabric flounced by a crinoline, and hearing "I'm in the Mood for Love" wafting up from the four-piece band below, I was filled with a breathless sense of expectation. I was fourteen years old.

I most remember the two-week stay at Robin Hood Inn that summer for my brief romance with the band's seventeen-year-old piano player, a Kirk Douglas look-alike named Dino Lorenzo. Why, one might wonder, with all the Jewish busboys and waiters available, did I fall for someone with the name of Dino Lorenzo? Ah, even then, I knew why. Not only was Kirk Douglas my absolute favorite movie star; I had, as they used to say, "a thing" for Italian piano players.

How important music was then; how much time we spent listening to records, learning songs, singing, playing. I had a pretty voice and was never shy about performing. But beyond that, I considered myself a real musician, having studied the accordion since I was eight. True, it was a bulky and clumsy instrument, but next best to a piano, for which there was clearly no room in our claustrophobic three-room apartment. But the effort it required! It had to be dragged out of its case, strapped on, pulled and manipulated before a sound came out. How I wished for the grace of a piano.

And here was Dino, a serious musician, going into his senior year at the High School of Performing Arts, who practiced classical music alone in the darkened casino every afternoon. But at night, as a member of the band, he created instant arrangements from a fake book to all the songs I loved and still connect to that summer: "Day by Day," "P.S. I Love You," "I Don't Stand a Ghost of a Chance with You," and in rumba tempo "Dream When You're Feelin' Blue"—all of which I later picked up on the accordion when I came home.

And then, he was Italian, the only non-Jewish culture I knew of at that time. To the Jewish kids in Bensonhurst, Italian was synonymous with Christian. We didn't know any others. My feeling that Italians were mysterious and exotic went back to my earliest encounters with them in kindergarten when I first heard the teacher call out their beautiful musical names: Rosemarie Bellafiore, Angelo Pierro, Maria Theresa Badalamente. Later I envied the little dark-haired girls who got dressed as brides in the spring for some mysterious thing called Holy Communion. As for Italian boys, we all felt they were different from Jewish boys, although we couldn't say how. Of course, it was understood and repeatedly underscored by my parents: they were clearly forbidden. But after all, this was the country, and it was only for two weeks.

Time away from home is somehow compressed: it seems there's more of it than actually exists. So it was with this romance, which was probably as much with the summer, the Mountains, and the music as it was with Dino. Still it was blissful, marred only by the guilt I endured over my cousin who waited on the porch for me each night so we could enter the room together and, I hoped, allay any suspicions my mother might have.

The two weeks passed, and we returned home. I never saw Dino again, although later that year I did see a picture of him in the *New York Post* with a group of other students who were going to perform at Carnegie Hall. I knew enough not to continue our relationship.

The boys in the band always held romantic appeal for young female guests — especially piano players who looked like Kirk Douglas.

Still, my mother must have had enough of an inkling of what went on not to want to risk a repeat. So after the summer of 1955, we never returned to the country together again.

ESTHER STRASSBERG: In the 1950s, my sister Irene Asman and I bought out our brothers and took over the running of Esther Manor. We catered to young families and attracted a lively crowd. Our slogan was "Big enough to serve you, small enough to know you."

Esther Manor did not have heat and was open only for the summer. I remember how sad it was when we closed up after Yom Kippur. We would take down the curtains to have them laundered for the following season, all the silver was polished and put away, and we moved out.

LEBA SEDAKA: My memories of Esther Manor go back to when it was a kind of farm—we had cows and chickens. I was still very young when they decided to stop raising animals. I had a pet calf and remember how despondent I was when it was taken away.

My mother ran Esther Manor. She worked harder than anyone I've ever seen. She'd be up until two or three in the morning, and at six she'd be in the kitchen again making sure everything was OK.

When I was very young, my mother would tell me I had to be very kind to the guests or else we would not be able to pay the mortgage. I had no idea what a mortgage was. It could have been some kind of monster. But I knew if a guest wanted my doll, I had to give it to her.

The hotel's capacity depended on how ambitious my mother was on any given weekend. She could get four to six people—sometimes couples—into one room. Oh yes! I would hide behind the switchboard when she went into action.

She'd tell people, "Now don't worry. I'll put up a screen. You're never going to be in the room anyway. You have two shows Saturday night, a cocktail hour, and a midnight show. There's no time to sleep. What do you care if someone's in the room?"

I never knew when I'd have my bed. Sometimes she would actually sell it, and I'd have to go into town to sleep, or she'd sell half my bed to a lady guest.

But I loved it, and I'd cry every Labor Day when the season came to an end. The summer I was thirteen, my grandfather was very ill, and the family worried he wouldn't make it through the summer. So my aunt and mother sent me, my sister, and my two cousins to a camp. It didn't work. The kids at camp went to sleep at the time I was used to getting dressed to go to a show at the hotel. I called home and cried. I was so upset. My mother said I'd have to stay. Finally I called my grandfather. "Papa, I can't take this. I have to come back." In twenty minutes, a car came for me.

ESTHER STRASSBERG: For the summer of 1958, we decided to hire an additional band at Esther Manor. We already had an orchestra, but we thought it would be nice to have a three-piece band to play around the pool during the day and in the nightclub at night so there would be continuous music.

On a weekend before the season began and school was still on, we had a convention group at the hotel. Saturday morning, my sister Irene and I were at the side of the pool with some gardeners planting flowers in a rock garden when these three boys came along.

"Can I help you?" I asked.

"Yes, we're your band," the shortest boy said. That was Norman Spizz.

"You're my band?" They looked like schoolboys. "Does your mother know you've left the city?"

"Yes. We're ready to begin work. Can we have our rooms?"

I didn't like these kids to begin with, but I said, "You're in Room 30. It has three beds."

"But we get three rooms."

"You get one room with three beds. If you care to have milk and cookies, go into the kitchen now and tell them that Esther sent you."

NEIL SEDAKA: When I first saw Esther, I thought she was six feet tall, she was so imposing. And we were very little, very green-looking, very young—all of nineteen years old. Our band was called the Nordanelles for Norman, David, and Neil. Norman Spizz was the trumpet player, David Bass played the bass, and I was the singing pianist. Later we added a sax player, Howard Tischler.

I later learned that Esther hit the ceiling when she saw us. She called Charlie Rapp, who had booked us, and complained, but he convinced her to give us a chance. Our first performance was actually an audition. Afterwards, all the guests came up to Esther to say how much they liked us.

ESTHER STRASSBERG: When everyone told me how terrific the trio was, I realized I had made a mistake by antagonizing the boys. We needed them. So at the end of the weekend, I went over to Norman Spizz. "No doubt we'll see you next weekend," I said.

"You won't see us next weekend," he answered.

But we did.

NEIL SEDAKA: That summer I played the accordion during the afternoon for the cha-cha lessons at the pool and at cocktail time. In the evenings our band played dance music and cut the show, as they used to say. Late at night we played in the cocktail lounge. We got paid $86.50 a week plus room and board.

It was a great summer for me, a great training ground. I was brought up in the Brighton Beach section of Brooklyn. Music had always been my life. For twelve years I studied at Juilliard under a piano scholarship. At the age of thirteen I was writing songs, performing in small bands, playing classical piano music. Still it was at Esther Manor that I learned to become a performer. I developed and grew there before audiences that were very tough but appreciative. You know, the hotel guests were paying for everything inclusive.

The crowd was basically young and hip because the hotel was near the Monticello Racetrack. A whole bunch of acts performed there who played the Mountains and nowhere else. Day, Dawn, and Dusk were three black guys who sang spirituals. The Magic Triplets, three delightful young men, did all kinds of singing and dancing. And then there were the big acts like Billy Eckstine and Totie Fields.

Esther never watched the shows but listened from her office through a little speaker while she did her paperwork late at night. The act that had the biggest impact was Totie Fields. All the guests went to Esther and told her how fabulous this new comedienne was.

I wasn't famous then. But I got the chance to do a lot of my early rock 'n' roll songs for the guests. I also tried to impress Esther's sixteen-year-old daughter, Leba.

LEBA SEDAKA: The first weekend Neil came up was the first time I saw him. I was behind the front desk when he walked by. Nothing happened, though, not at that moment. He came over to me and said, "Hi, my name is Neil Sedaka, and I wrote a song for Connie Francis."

And I said, "That's absolutely ridiculous. I never knew anyone who would write songs."

"Listen to the radio," he said. "I wrote a song called 'Stupid Cupid,' and Connie Francis recorded it."

Of course, I didn't believe him until I heard it on the radio. When Neil returned with his friends the next weekend, I told him "I heard that song, and it's very good."

"I told you," he said. "I write songs."

NEIL SEDAKA: That summer I began to date Leba. We'd go to the movies in Loch Sheldrake or to a place across from the racetrack for ice cream sodas.

LEBA SEDAKA: Esther Manor was set back on a bit of a hill, but the casino was on the road. A wonderful path with a couple of benches along the way led down to it. Neil and I would take lovely walks on that road. We spent a lot of our time together on the grounds. My mom wanted me to stay on the property as much as possible. She didn't like the way people drove cars in the summer, and she didn't want me to go to the other hotels. She thought if I were seen, people would wonder if there was something wrong with our place.

That summer of '58 "It's All in the Game" was popular, and it became our song. Later on Neil included it in one of his albums for that first summer we were together.

NEIL SEDAKA: I remember that summer working at Esther Manor and trying along with my friends to sneak into other hotels to see the shows. The Concord was the most difficult place to get into if you weren't a guest. It was scary having to pass by that menacing front booth with all its security. And if your name was not on the list you couldn't get by. You had to know someone. My "in" was Carl Goldstein, the attorney for the Concord and the Parkers and also Esther's brother. Thanks to Uncle Carl I remember seeing some fabulous shows.

A few years later, I played the Concord. I didn't play it again for many, many years. Not that I didn't do well, but the booker Phil Greenwald didn't like me for some reason. We just didn't get along very well.

I remember going to see a show at the Concord and sitting ringside. Milton Berle was performing, and we were all so much in awe of him. To my amazement, in the middle of the show, Milton introduced me to the audience. I was thrilled to pieces, and just over the moon. I took a bow and thought maybe Phil Greenwald will take notice of me now. But he never did. Twenty-five or thirty years later, Milton Berle opened for me two or three times at the Riviera Hotel in Las Vegas. So I had gone full circle.

LINDA HOPKINS: I did a number of shows at Esther Manor that summer of 1958, and that's where I first met Neil Sedaka. Every song he wrote was with Leba in mind. "I'm going to pray that you and Leba get married one day," I told him. And he said, "Please do pray."

LEBA SEDAKA: My father was crazy about Neil from the start. He used to say, "That boy is a genius." Although my mom liked Neil very much as a person, she had reservations about him as a potential son-in-law. He played the piano. He was a klezmer, a musician. My aunts and uncles objected to him. They wanted me to go out with future doctors or lawyers. To this day, Neil has not gotten over that. When he has a major accomplishment, he still asks, "Would your doctor or lawyer have been able to do that?"

NEIL SEDAKA: It was after that summer of 1958 that I recorded my first hit, "The Diary." Leba was still a student at Monticello High, and she took on the job of answering my fan mail.

There was a small-town attitude among the young people who lived in the Mountains that was very different from New York City. I had graduated from Lincoln High School in a class of 2,000. Monticello High had just a few hundred students. When Leba and I went to her high school prom, it was just after I had done Dick Clark's "American Bandstand," a big national TV show. All the high school kids there seemed jealous and smirky over the fact that I was a rock 'n' roll star.

In 1961, Leba and I became engaged, and we got married the following year in the card room at Esther Manor. But the reception was at the Concord.

LEBA SEDAKA: The reason for having the reception at the Concord was that I knew if it were at our hotel my mother would be jumping up and down and probably wind up in the kitchen.

"Thinking back now I realize that Esther Manor and the Catskills were a great boost not only to my career but to my life. It was there that I learned how to perform and where I fell in love" — Neil Sedaka. Engagement photo of Neil Sedaka and Leba Strassberg, 1961.

ESTHER STRASSBERG: After Neil became a star he came back once to play at Esther Manor. He didn't charge us; I couldn't have afforded him anyway.

Through the years I always went downstairs to my little office and listened to the entertainers on loudspeakers. I was never interested in what the entertainers did—only in the applause, the bravos. But that night, I left my office and went to the nightclub. And when I saw Neil on stage, I was touched.

"I can't believe it's Neil," I said to my husband. "My little man."

The Bauer Sisters, famed golfers, "get a leg up" on the Grossinger golf course.

NEIL SEDAKA: The guys in the band that I played with at Esther Manor are all scattered today. Howie Tischler became a dentist. David Bass lives in Florida. I don't know what he does, but he's not in show business. Norman Spizz books bands and entertainment for a firm. Only I lived out the dream.

NORMAN HANOVER: The Catskills, to me, was a dreamworld. I came from a neighborhood in the Bronx where I could hear the Jerome Avenue el rumble by and shake things in my apartment. I'd wake up in the summer mornings with a pillow full of sweat. There were no air conditioners, no fans other than a window fan. But you'd go up to the Mountains and you could walk on grass.

The Pineview in Fallsburg was one of the major hotels for Orthodox Jews—very traditional-looking, white. To keep up, they added on newer buildings, and it was like an octopus with arms coming off the main building.

The Pineview was owned and run by generations of the Liebowitz family. I worked there for a couple of summers in the early '60s, and I was everything from a counselor to a teaboy to a busboy.

The old lady, Mrs. Liebowitz, a big heavyset woman, would walk around with a fly swatter. She was almost like a fullback, and whenever she came around, people would say "Watch out!" She set the tone even though she was in her late eighties. And it was passed on to her sons who were in their fifties and sixties. One son ran the food operation. He was tough as nails and handled the difficult situation of workers who would go out and get drunk every payday and then destroy things. The other son handled reservations and ran the hotel.

Groups of people would sit under a tree on the old-style lawn chairs or on the porch on the Adirondack chairs and would be called

Basketball was so hot at Tamarack that they played it in the pool.

out by the social director over the public address system to do the cha-cha. People loved it. There were also some very competitive basketball games. The Pineview team would travel to other hotels to play, and some of the guests would go along to cheer them on.

That was the milieu. There was another part, too. People waited all year to get up for two weeks, or a month—some even stayed the full two months. And they demanded blood. That's what it was: blood. They were king of the hill. They were the boss. They were paying good money, and they wanted everything. And they got so demanding that sometimes the situation was brutal. You got it from the guests. You were under the gun from the owners. You were under the gun from your fellow workers.

In the tearoom after the show late at night, people would come in for a fifth course—hot prune juice or tea and cookies—as if they didn't get enough food. And we had to serve them again. Somehow I got hooked up with this incredible character who said, "We're going to charge them."

"You've got to be crazy," I told him. "The old lady with the fly swatter is constantly around. How will you ever be able to explain that you're charging for something that's free?"

"We're doing it."

It was outrageous, but the guests paid. What was amazing to me was that this was a hotel where people returned year after year and knew the rules, but it was possible to get away with something even with them.

The background of the guests was very moral, very ethical. They were Orthodox Jewish families at a time in the late '50s and early '60s. One could meet young women, but they were always with their families and there was no privacy. But at four in the morning, one could see waiters rushing out of a guest room in their black pants and white shirts, sneaking down a fire escape.

The kitchen was hot and grueling. It was fast and you had to run out different courses, and waiters kept cutting the lines to get their orders. The owners had a family chauffeur who would drive into Fallsburg or Monticello and bring back the *New York Times* or certain mail. This man had been with the family for decades and thought he owned the place. One day he came into the kitchen and put his finger into a bowl of soup to taste. And the Chinese chef took his spatula and cut the chauffeur's chin so bad it was bleeding like wild—right in the middle of serving lunch. The owner's son had to come in and referee.

What I experienced, the guests never saw: substandard living quarters for the staff; the treatment of the help; learning to eat what had been eaten, like the dozens of one-tenth-eaten baby lamb chops from the children's dining room that we made a meal of; the tensions on payday when we'd scramble to get out of the hotel and be free to go into town and have a good time.

Still, of course, I have wonderful feelings for the area. That is where I grew up. I did not grow up in the Bronx in a four-flight walk-up with my parents who were immigrants to this country. What I learned, I learned there. Whether it's sex, whether it's business, whether it's the wise guy-ness of that character charging in the tea-room, or the brutality of some of the guests, whether it's the jokes, the getting along, the fabulous Mountain earnings giving me the means to get an education and make it—to all of us who worked there as young people, going up to the Catskills was an awakening of unbelievable proportions.

PETER ROTHHOLZ: My introduction to America came through the Catskills in one of those hotels typical of the "era," although it was a few years before that time. I came from Germany originally, but we all moved to England before the Second World War. My parents were divorced, and I remained with my father in England when my mother and stepfather came to the United States. So immediately after the end of the war in Europe, I came to America to be with them.

I arrived in New York on May 24, 1945. It was the beginning of summer here, and I remember very shortly thereafter my mother saying, "Well, you know people in America get a job for the summer. What are you going to do?" I was not aware of that. You don't have long summer vacations in England.

I said, "What kind of jobs do people get?"

She said, "Well, if I were you, I'd try to get something in the country."

Friends in New York invited me over one day after I had been here a week or two. And I asked one of them, "I'm supposed to get a job for the summer, and my mother says the country would be a good thing. What does she mean? What is the country? Where is the country? What kind of a job could I get?"

And he said, "I know just the thing for you. Let me call. Because I worked my way all through college and dental school at a resort in the Catskills." He explained it to me, and he called these people up. They said sure and wanted to know what I could do. I had absolutely no idea. But anyway I was hired as a bellhop. I can't remember the

Peter Rothholz (second from right) was introduced to America at a small Catskill hotel, the Edgewood Inn in Livingston Manor.

owners' name, but the resort was the Edgewood Inn. They advertised "Edgewood Inn—Your Country Estate in Livingston Manor."

At the end of June, I turned sixteen. A few days later, I took the bus from the Dixie Hotel on West 42nd Street—there was a bus terminal there in those days—up to the country. I didn't know where I was going or what I was getting into. I arrived at the place. It was quite nice, a good-sized hotel—it must have had a couple of hundred rooms, a main building, some cottages, a big lake. They had a lot of help, but many of them were young women or young men like myself, because remember this was the summer of 1945 when most young men eighteen or over were in the military.

The Edgewood Inn had horses for riding, and I was quartered above the stables, which I rather liked. They sort of explained to me what I had to do, and it wasn't too difficult.

At the time, I had very much of an English public school accent— an upper-class accent, I still had most of my English clothes, and my English attitudes. So I was quite distinctive. And that made for some advantages and also some problems.

Because of my speech pattern, I quickly got a job in addition to my other duties. They had a PA system: "Mrs. Ginzberg, please come to the telephone." "Mr. Paul, there is a message waiting for you." "Dinner tonight will be served at 7 P.M." Anyway, because of the way I sounded, they put me on the PA system, and everybody thought this was the most phenomenal thing imaginable. It sounded like a BBC voice on there. I became a little bit of a celebrity.

In England, we were not rich by any means—in fact, we were quite poor. But when all the children were sent to the countryside for the war, I ended up in Cambridge, and so I went to this very fancy public school. And one of the things that they teach you there is that money is sort of crass, vulgar.

Now here, at the Edgewood Inn, I was supposed to be working for tips. I didn't quite know how to handle that kind of thing. I carried up the bags because it was a nice thing to do for people. It didn't seem right to collect money for doing that, so I would take off before I had a chance to get any tips.

As time went on, though, I learned to accept tips. I realized that I did have to take some money because that's what I was there for. Once someone gave me $3. I thought that was an awful lot of money, but I took it. I learned about the territoriality that came with the

bellhop's job, such as the card game concession. On a rainy day when they couldn't sit around the lake, people would want to have a card game in the lounge. The bellhop would set up the game, bring in the card tables and the chairs. And we got an extra tip for that.

I had grown up in a Jewish environment in England. I had a large family, and the school I attended had a lot of Jewish boys, but the Jewish culture here was totally different. The food was different. I never had seen a bagel or pastrami before. Also, people behaved differently here, and that took some getting used to. Where I grew up, people tended to be quiet. They had fun but without being so loud. Here there was always a lot of noise and tumult. There was even a tummler—what the French call an *animateur*, someone who created excitement in a crowd.

There were all sorts of entertainers in the shows at night, but to me the most unusual was the mind reader. I had never been exposed to one before, and I never forgot him. I believe his name was The Magnificent Polgar or something like that. He became quite famous.

I have some fond memories of that summer. The family that owned the hotel were very nice people, and I remember them very warmly. I thought the countryside was quite lovely and the lake very appealing. I had always liked boats and boating, and on my free time I would take a canoe and go out on the lake by myself. On my day off, I'd go with some of the other people into Livingston Manor to a movie—a musical more often than not—and then we'd go to a soda fountain. I was fascinated by soda fountains. I was also fascinated by the cars. In England there wasn't anything like them. There was a sense of plenty to America that I wasn't used to. No one seemed to be deprived of anything. I was also up in the country for VJ Day, when the Japanese surrendered, and that was a wonderful time.

But to be honest with you, it was the summer of my discontent. Everything was so fresh, and I was just really out of it. I didn't know about girls yet, which was stupid of me because girls found me attractive as I was different. I made only passing, fleeting friendships. I had been very close to my father, and I missed him a great deal.

The great disappointment was that I had a picture of America as a sort of paradise. Because my mother lived in the United States, I would talk to GIs, and they also spoke of home as a paradise. But it was their paradise, not mine. Don't forget how fortunate I had been. I had not been hungry, oppressed, persecuted. Even though I wasn't born English, I fit in perfectly by the time I had lived there for a few years. For all intents and purposes, I was an English kid, and now for all intents and purposes, I was a foreigner.

Still, it was the first real job I ever had—I even had to get a social security card in Livingston Manor—and I took home about $145 at the end of the summer. As it turned out, I remained in the United States, and I always think of the Catskills as my introduction to America.

Busy night and day: the switchboard at the Raleigh.

JEFF KROLICK: I began in the Catskills as a thirteen-year-old piano player in a bungalow colony. My first appearance, I played the accompaniment for a stripper.

"We're going to do 'Hello, Dolly!' " she said.

"What key?"

"Honey, I'm not singing it."

My parents were in the audience that night. I don't think they liked the idea of my playing for a stripper too much. But the show had to go on.

ERROL DANTE: At the bungalow colony the attitude was always "If you're so good, why are you working here?" By the time you got there it would be one, two in the morning. You'd walk in through those torn screen doors. They'd all had some drinks. There'd be a bottle on every table.

SAL RICHARDS: Oh, those bungalow colonies. The hot dressing rooms—no air conditioning, of course. You change in the back. People peek in through a broken window. The heat on stage when you're working.

In most of those places there were no spotlights, just lights stuck into the ceiling. I was performing at the SGS Bungalows near the Stevensville Hotel, opened my mouth to sing, and a giant moth flew in. I almost choked. I spit the moth out.

"That moth," I told the audience, "does that every week. He loves that song."

VIC ARNELL: If you tried to get from an early show to a late show on a Saturday night, it was almost impossible because the roads were so jammed with cars running from one hotel to another to see shows. The people were just running for entertainment. A person spending a summer there at that time could have seen 75 to 100 different performers.

ELLIOT FINKEL: I spent a lot of my childhood in the New Edgewood Hotel in Loch Sheldrake. It was a fleabag with no bathrooms except for a shack out in the back like an outhouse. There were always bugs, and the food was lousy. Everyone knew it was a dump, but it was always jammed because the owner spent a fortune on entertainment. There were always two shows a night. Henny Youngman played there. Georgie Jessel was there, and all the stars of the Yiddish theater.

The owner, Garfinkel, would get so caught up in what he was doing that he would put big ads in the newspapers: "Fisherman's Paradise"—the lake was mostly swamp; "Olympic Swimming Pool"—it was four feet deep. He advertised the great stars that were to appear there.

My mother would call him. "I see you're advertising Jennie Goldstein."

"Yes, that's right."

"But she died last year."

"So . . . ? What's the difference?"

SOL ZIM: The New Edgewood was one of the "low end" places I worked in when I was trying to break in as an entertainer. I'm a kind of "Jazz Singer" with a twist: started out as a cantor and became a pop singer—but managed to combine both. Because I was known as a cantor, it was hard to get a start as an entertainer. I was "too Jewish" for the big places. So my brother and I worked maybe sixty shows a summer, in every kochalayn, every little cabana place up there.

At the New Edgewood, Garfinkel would advertise me as appearing there for Passover: "The Great Cantor." But I didn't have to show up, didn't have to do the seders. All I'd have to do is one concert over the whole holiday, with no piano. That's how he covered himself. "I make my whole Pesach on you," he'd say.

That was one of the places I crossed off my list when I started moving up. Another was a place that when I walked in, the owner came out in bare feet and said, "Oh, you're doing the show tonight? Okay, in there." He pointed to the casino. "Someone's going to play the music for you."

I said, "But I'm supposed to have a band."

"They couldn't make it. We only have a piano player."

I went into the casino. The piano had less than a full keyboard. Not only that, but out of the forty-eight keys, maybe twenty-five of them worked.

Another place was the Echo Lodge, up on a little hill not far from Tamarack. We'd go there about four times a summer. It was higher

Sol Zim, who has appeared as both cantor and pop singer at many Catskill resorts, at the Stevensville Hotel, Passover 1962.

than a kochalayn, but lower than a lodge. I'd go nuts. The piano player couldn't read music. They didn't have any rooms, so we had to sleep on cots on the stage.

MAL Z. LAWRENCE: I started out as a social director at the Sunrise Manor in Ellenville, guest capacity: 250–300. This was 1955. I took women on walks, did Simon Sez. The first time I did Simon Sez, I gave away thirty T-shirts; I couldn't get anyone out.

The owner was a tough and frugal guy named Kramer. He had keys to every room and would make the rounds every night. If you were on staff and had a light on after midnight, he'd open the door. "No lights burning after twelve," he'd say. "I pay for it."

Once a woman guest walked over to him. "Mr. Kramer," she said, "I can't sleep on one pillow. I need two."

He looked her straight in the eye. "I sleep on one pillow. You'll sleep on one pillow."

FREDDIE ROMAN: My grandfather always went to the Paramount Hotel in Parksville. It's an example of what's always been best in small Catskill hotels, owned all along by the Gasthalter family.

MAL Z. LAWRENCE: I played the Paramount in the late 1950s when the dressing rooms were closets. A performer had to share space with the bingo game, the rack for the limbo dance, the amplifier, and dozens of assorted props. The nail and the wall—that was the dressing room.

The Paramount was open all year, and it could get cold in the winter. Once I worked there over a Christmas vacation. You had to walk out of the hotel and through the snow to get to the playhouse, the only place in the hotel large enough to stage a show.

This night, people were complaining as they shlepped and traipsed through the snow, kicking it off their boots and shoes as they entered the playhouse. Before you knew it, there was a flood. Water was everywhere. Guests had to move further and further away from the door, and closer and closer to the stage.

Finally, the singer came out on stage. She took the microphone and let out a shriek. The wire from the mike must have had a crack in it. She got the shock of her life. The place went wild. And all this, just from a bunch of people shaking the snow off their boots.

Doing the turkey trot, in a 1950s publicity shot.

FREIDA BAKER: I came to the Paramount in 1956 to play the piano for the evening, and I've been here ever since. I think I'm the only woman bandleader in the Catskills. My band has a trumpet player, a drummer, and a violinist—that's my husband. Our band has an old feeling. When we first began, he would play a lot of Hungarian Gypsy music, but there isn't too much of a call for that kind of stuff anymore.

SOL ZIM: Arnold Graham booked us at the Paramount, but we didn't stay for long. The owner, Freddie Gasthalter, came in while I was setting up my PA system. Here I was, having shlepped up the whole system and tipped a bellhop $15 to help me put it together with all the wires, and Freddie says, "You can't use your system. You have to use mine. We have our own system. It's fantastic."

I said, "But we're a duo. You only have one mike."

He said, "Then you'll both sing out of one mike."

We had to stand there, singing cheek to cheek.

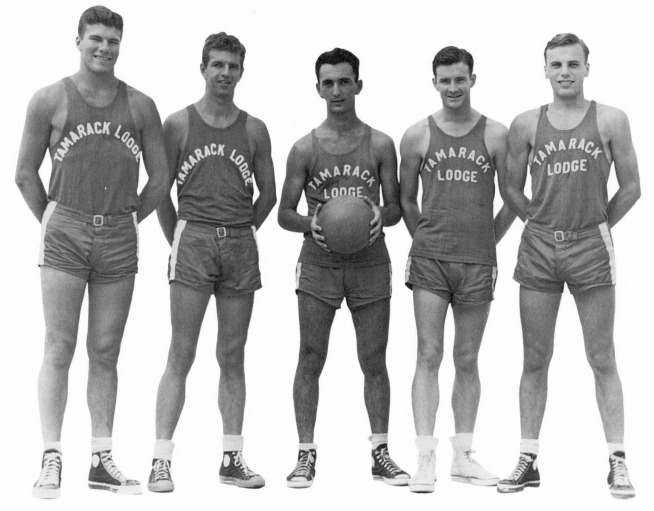

Tamarack Lodge's basketball team in the 1950s included (left to right): Ed Leede, Ed Redding, Bob Cousy, Frank Offtring, and Wes Fields.

MILTON KUTSHER: Dancing cheek to cheek and playing basketball head to head are some of the images that stay with me when I think of the "era."

We started getting into basketball around 1950. It gave us a new dimension. It was a morale booster for the staff and gave the guests something to root for.

RALPH GREENBERG: Tamarack went out for basketball in a big way especially after the war. The guys who played or coached for Tamarack over the years included Allie Sherman, Max Zaslofsky, Sid Tannenbaum, and Bob Cousy. There was no clock then, no time limit, and Cousy could dribble the heck out of the ball—no one could take it away from him. He was a weapon for us.

We played two games a week, one home and one away, a Friday night and a Sunday. We had a lot of famous refs like Lou Eisenstein, one of the top officials in college ball for years, and we paid them $15 a game. All the guests and staff came out to watch. At Tamarack, we even had a grandstand built. All the hotel teams had uniforms. Ours were green and white.

DAVE LEVINSON: Our team meant a lot to me. We often played against the Nevele. Their players were mostly from NYU, and they would go to the trouble to get Howard Cann, their coach, to come up and coach and try to defeat us.

RALPH GREENBERG: The Nevele, as far as I can remember, had the closest thing to ringers. They were loaded there. They had guys who were college graduates, who in the winter months were playing as semipros.

LOU GOLDSTEIN: It was common practice for Catskill hotel teams to be made up of college teams. Milton Kutsher had the University of Kentucky basketball team: Cliff Hagan—great players, guys who later went into the pros and became members of the Indianapolis Olympians. The Ambassador had the Bradley basketball team. Klein's Hillside had George Mikan and some other DePaul University players.

RALPH GREENBERG: Everybody on the hotel teams—with rare exceptions—worked bellhop or dining staff. It wasn't a scholarship program, but college coaches called up hotels asking for jobs for their athletes. They wanted their kids playing here to get the experience.

DAVE LEVINSON: For quite a few years Tamarack played an all-star team from the other hotels picked by newspapermen for the Damon Runyon cancer fund. One year we went up against a team with a bunch of top players including Wilt Chamberlain from Kutsher's. We went into overtime, once, maybe twice even. We finally lost the game. And Bob Cousy sat down and cried. We didn't realize that these games meant so much to our waiters and busboys.

MILTON KUTSHER: Wilt Chamberlain worked as a bellhop in the early '50s, while he was still going to Overbrook High School in Philadelphia. He was so thin and stringy, you wouldn't even recognize him, but he could play basketball.

When I got Wilt, I was looking around for the right coach to work with him. There was a couple, a tailor and his wife, who had been

"He was so thin and stringy, you wouldn't recognize him. But he could play basketball." — Milton Kutsher on Wilt Chamberlain.

The long and short of it: Wilt Chamberlain as bellhop at Kutsher's in the 1950s.

coming to Kutsher's for years. One day, we got to talking. "You know, Mr. Kutsher," the man said, "my son was with the Washington Capitols. They won a championship, but then the team got disbanded. I bet he could help your team as a coach."

"Sure," I said. "Let him give me a call. Maybe we can work something out."

That's how I got Red Auerbach to coach Kutsher's basketball team. Red then was like he's been through all the years—he hasn't changed a great deal—pugnacious. He didn't take any stuff from anybody.

I still remember a game against the Brickman Hotel. Red got on their team so much that a fight broke out. The owner of Brickman's came running out. "Call the police. Arrest that Red Auerbach," he shouted.

Things calmed down, and, if I remember correctly, we won. We won a lot of games with Red Auerbach. He was always worth an extra five to ten points.

MARVIN WELKOWITZ: The Fishmans, who owned Young's Gap Hotel, were very involved with basketball, and when they hired busboys and waiters the most important questions they asked were, "Where did you play your ball? How tall are you? Can you shoot? Can you dribble?"

They did this because part of their profile was fielding a top-level basketball team. Young's Gap played its games at 10, 11 o'clock at night, tournaments against other hotels. Nobody could beat them. The lobby was decorated with pictures of famous basketball players who went on to star in college and in professional basketball.

RALPH GREENBERG: There was always a lot of action and plenty of bets. People would take numbers in a pool to guess the total score of a game going up to 200. It was a dollar a person. There never was too much money bet, maybe $175 maximum.

LOU GOLDSTEIN: It was sometimes common practice for teams to split a bet with a guest. When we reached the bet score, say 95 points, we would freeze the ball. And then we would split with the guests fifty-fifty. But teams didn't throw games, they threw scores.

When the college basketball scandals hit in the early 1950s because of teams actually throwing games, the NCAA stepped in and stopped all the schools from playing for and at the hotels. Basketball didn't die in the Mountains, but the ruling did end all that great head-to-head, hotel-to-hotel basketball competition.

DAVE LEVINSON: Some of the enterprising Catskill people got involved in another venture, the Monticello Racetrack. We decided to build in 1952. There was one franchise available in the State of New York. I was approached by Sidney Sussman from the Windsor Hotel along with Morris Abraham, who was president of the hotel association. I came up with the money to lobby for the track. We bought 250 acres. Sidney, Paul Grossinger, Bob Stapleton (a lawyer in Ellenville), and I were the founders. Then Ben Slutsky came on the board, and Stapleton begged off. We needed more money and we gave directorships to people like Milton Kutsher who came up with money. We ended up with about sixteen directors. The first summer was rough, but after that we got off the ground and did great. In 1985, we sold out to Buddy Berenson, who's operating it today.

Gambling has always been part of our life-style. It gave the Mountains employment and Monticello a lot in taxes. To this day, Tuesday

A high-wheeled sulky on parade the day the Monticello Racetrack opened.

is racetrack day. The buses line up, take 400, 500 people from the hotels.

All of the help deposit their money there. Our chef at Tamarack, who had been with us for twenty years, deposited *all* his money there. When I sold the hotel, I made arrangements for all the employees to stay, but he decided to move on. He went to Brown's, then to the Raleigh, getting half the salary I used to pay him.

Somebody asked him, "Sam, aren't you sorry? You could have stayed at Tamarack." He said, "What difference does it make? I wind up with the same money every year."

JULIE SLUTSKY: It was natural for the Nevele to get involved in the Monticello Racetrack. We've always had riding stables, and when I was ten, my father put me in charge of them. I had to get up very early in the morning to feed and care for the horses. I remember how I used to pray for rain so I could get a little more sleep. I'd go to the Ulster County Fair in Ellenville, take part in the harness racing and the games like going to Jerusalem—a version of musical chairs—on horseback. I think that's when I developed my lifelong love of horses.

We're the only Catskill hotel with its own racing stable—Nevele Acres, which we started in the 1960s. Stanley Dancer trained and raced for us. There were several years of buying, selling, dreams that went bust, aggravation. One day Stanley told me a woman had a horse to sell for $20,000. I took a look at him. You know, all those horses are beautiful; they all look like world-beaters. Stanley Dancer recommended purchase, however, so we went along with his judgment. The horse was sired by Worthy Pride so we named him Nevele Pride. All our horses have the name Nevele. The first time Nevele Pride raced, he won two heats at Goshen. We knew he had something. Nevele Pride became one of the fastest trotters in history. He won fifty-seven of sixty-seven starts and was one of the all-time top money winners in harness racing. His record for the half mile lasted twenty years. Every time Nevele Pride won, we got the capital to finance development and improvement for the hotel. We needed that horse. We sold him to stud for $3 million.

We've always had some pretty good horses: Nevele Rascal, Nevele Big Shot, and Nevele Diamond. But I don't think there'll ever be an equal to Nevele Pride.

DICK KITTRELL: Everyone was talking about the Nevele the summer of 1966, when President Lyndon B. Johnson visited the Catskills to dedicate a hospital in Ellenville. His helicopter landed on the grounds of the hotel, and he spent the night. Security forces were stationed all around the area to guard him. Traffic was halted along Routes 209 and 52 from Ellenville all the way to the towns of Kingston, Wurtsboro, Walden, and Woodbourne.

At that time, my wife, Miriam, and our son, Gary, were in Woodbourne, where we used to spend the summer when the kids were little, and I remember that summer as the time Miriam overcame the resistance of crack army troops and passed through their ranks at Neversink River Bridge.

Our son, who was four years old then, wasn't feeling well, and Miriam decided a visit to the doctor was in order. Undeterred by the sight of men in uniform, she bundled the boy into the car and headed off toward Dr. Martin Rubin's office on the far side of the Neversink Bridge. At the edge of town, she was stopped by troops standing guard by the foot of the bridge. Miriam got out of the car and engaged the soldiers in a heated discussion which was accompanied by much hand waving and finger pointing and ended with a summons to the captain commanding the force.

After conversing briefly with Miriam, the captain signaled his men to allow the vehicle to pass, whereupon Miriam got back in her car and, breaking through army lines, drove across the bridge to an old two-story building just beyond to keep her appointment.

Gary recovered quickly. Miriam was vindicated. Everyone at Kassack's Bungalow Colony remarked on her dauntlessness and courage. President Johnson, upon hearing of the captain's action, commended him publicly for his humanitarian gesture. And I never did believe the rumor that persisted all summer that the President, enraged at the breach in his security, secretly ordered the captain to be sent to Vietnam the next day.

MARVIN WELKOWITZ: In the early '60s when I was twelve, I moved to the Ridge Mountain Hotel off Revonah Hill Road in Parksville. The place was originally developed by my grandparents Max and Rose Welkowitz and was then taken over by my parents, Joel and Sara.

The hotel was on a high ridge about 2,100 feet above sea level. On a clear day you can see twenty-four miles out; on a very sharp

ABOVE AND FOLLOWING PAGE: **Not by** mambo alone — golfing and sunbathing during the "era."

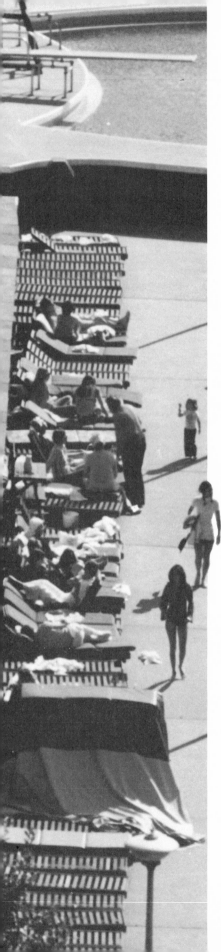

day with a good pair of binoculars you can see almost as far as New Paltz, almost forty miles.

Most of the places in the area were not year-round, but in the summer it was booming. There'd be about 2,000 people from the hotels and the bungalow colonies, not to mention Grossinger's, swelling the streets of the Town of Liberty. People came up for a week or two, and the small hotels didn't have concession stands or shops, so guests would walk around and shop.

MAL Z. LAWRENCE: In those days, towns like Liberty, Monticello, and Fallsburg were jammed at night. Today you don't see people on the streets, but then, it seemed everyone went out at night. It was cool, pleasant to go for a walk, eat an ice cream cone, go see a movie. There were always lines waiting to get into the movies.

MARVIN WELKOWITZ: A mile away from us was the Grand Hotel run by Maxie Schmidt and his wife. Then you had the Klass Hotel. Right across from that was the New Brighton Hotel run by Archie Morgenstern. Toward Parksville you had Klein's Hillside, a little bit bigger than ours. We held about 200 people, they had almost 350. Not even a mile from the Paramount was the Tanzville Hotel. I was friendly with Jay, the son of the owner. We were the same age. We had staff softball teams and would play against each other.

Young's Gap was right near us, but it was a larger hotel in the 700 capacity range. It evolved from Ma and Pa Holder to a partnership named Spector and Ginsberg. Young's Gap was the only place in the area open year-round. It was one of the first hotels in Sullivan County to have an indoor pool, and that became their trademark, their selling point. It helped them attract a very young crowd.

BARRY FOX: I was fortunate enough to catch the tail end of the "era." Every night something was doing: a showcase at Brickman's, a late show at the Laurels, all the maitre d's meeting at the pizza place in Monticello, trading stories.

BOB FELDMAN: The Eldorado near Old Falls, in Fallsburg—capacity about 600. For years the place was known as Zeiger's, but after it went bankrupt in 1957, the Slutskys, cousins of the people who own the Nevele, bought it and renamed it the Eldorado.

The Slutskys remodeled the nightclub into the first tiered one in the area. I was in charge of booking the acts and the bar. Lillian Roth was making a comeback then, and she was our first act. I booked rock shows every Tuesday night—the Drifters, the Toys, groups like that.

Soon the lounge became a hangout for every act in the Mountains. They would perform for nothing after the late shows. And it seemed like every married, as well as every single, woman showed up. The place would get so jammed, it was impossible to get in. One night Phil Greenwald came down with Alan Sherman, the guy who did "Hello Muddah, Hello Faddah." We had no place to put them. The Eldorado was standing room only, blasting music, funny shtiks, action going on till five in the morning. And the funny thing was that the hotel itself didn't do much business. It was empty most of the time.

MARVIN SCOTT: My grandmother had been a guest at the Raleigh Hotel for several seasons, and in 1958 I was coming up on college and wanting a summer job. My grandmother put in the word, and I had a job as a bellhop.

During that era there was a family crowd at the Raleigh with a couple of swingers coming in occasionally to check out the hotel. The bellhops were the elite of the staff. We had uniforms. I still recall the burgundy jacket I wore with all the buttons down the front. I must have looked like Johnny from the old Philip Morris commercial.

We bellhops were the first image of the place to the guests coming in, and we were always coached about how important it was to be courteous and well groomed. In those nice uniforms, we stood tall or paraded back and forth in the lobby.

Working at the Raleigh exposed me to a lot of different things for the first time. One of them was a professional stripper; let's just call her Nanette. She worked the 52nd Street joints in Manhattan between Fifth and Sixth. In those years there was a whole range of jazz and strip joints in that area. She came up to the Raleigh for a vacation and a little rest.

In the lobby there were signs like PLEASE DO NOT WALK THROUGH LOBBY IN BATHING ATTIRE. Well, fully dressed, Nanette came through the lobby wearing less than what one would wear in bathing attire. And all the young bellhops and other staff members just ogled her, fantasized about her.

"My grandmother put in the word, and I had a job as a bellhop at the Raleigh" — Marvin Scott.

One night I was up at the bar having some drinks and, incredibly, Nanette came over to me. We were talking and drinking, drinking and talking. All these men came around to her, making a big play. Suddenly, a guy says, "Nanette, let me take you back to your room."

And she says, "No, that's not necessary. He's taking me."

I took a look around. The "he" was me. I was so frightened. "Just a minute, Nanette," I said. "I've got to go to the men's room."

I raced back down to our den where the staff slept and woke up my best friend. "Quick, give me some condoms."

"What the hell are you waking me up for?" he cried. "What do you need them for?"

"I'm getting together with Nanette."

"Bull!"

He didn't believe me. I don't know if *I* believed me.

I went with Nanette to her room, Room 511 in the Sammy Davis Wing. Some things you never forget. And there I was in this plush room with this voluptuous woman who I had dreamed about. Talk about fantasies. When night turned into daybreak, we called for room service.

My best friend came down delivering the tray. Of course, he had no idea of who was in the room. As he was leaving I peeked out from under the covers. "Boy, there's a nice tip for you on the dresser," I said.

Shocked, he let out a couple of expletives, took the juice and poured it into the coffee, and left—along with the tip.

Nanette and I became friendly, and every time I was off from bellhopping duties during the course of the week we'd spend time together. Eventually, she went back to New York City to ply her trade, and I never saw her again. But I'll never forget her. That experience with Nanette was my baptism. Like for many other teenagers, the Catskills was for me a crossing over from adolescence to adulthood, from innocence to exposure to real life.

MAL Z. LAWRENCE: The mid '50s into the '60s—that was the best time. It was mambo time. Mambo was hot. People had money to spend, went away more. There were the cars in shining bright colors; each year they got bigger and more elaborate—Cadillacs with big pointed fenders, Chevy Impalas, Thunderbirds, Mustangs. It was all flash, a glamorous and glittering time.

MARVIN SCOTT: It was the time of the Cadillac Eldorado. The colors don't stand out so much as the car itself; it was so big and good-looking, elegant, plush.

MAL Z. LAWRENCE: It was the time of nightlife. All over the Mountains, hotels had Mambo Night—the Raleigh was famous for theirs—and dancing would go on till seven in the morning. You had to fight to get in. You had to know somebody to get in.

People got all dressed up. Women wore elegant dresses, beautiful gowns; men wore suits and ties. A lot of the male performers, and guests too, wore the Machito shirts: big blousy things, with white cuffs sticking out of the suit jacket.

I would be there at the Raleigh. They would call me up on stage, and I'd do two or three dirty jokes, raunchy jokes. Then I'd sing "Old Black Magic." The song I used to like was "Pupapino, pupopino, pupapap papapino, pa ap pa pa ap pa."

JACK EAGLE: Latin music was created by the Cubans and Puerto Ricans, but somehow the Jewish people became addicted to it. Every hotel had a mambo teacher.

ERROL DANTE: Latin was, in a way, what disco is today. But it was such a joy, such infectious music. The Catskills became a mecca for Latin music.

CEIL BECKMAN JACOBS: I think my late husband, Al Beckman, played a big part in bringing about the Latin music craze in the Catskills. We met in 1938 on a liquor dealer's cruise from Nassau to Havana. On that trip, Al fell in love with me. He also fell in love with Havana: the Sans Souci, the swans on little lakes, the gorgeous showgirls silhouetted against the sky in open-air theaters. Al was so enchanted by the beat and sound of Latin music, he brought it back to the United States. He started booking Latin bands and dancers in the Mountains. After the war he opened a club in Loch Sheldrake with a Latin flavor. I can still hear the four-piece rumba group, the clicking heels of the famous Spanish dancers who appeared there. Rumba, samba—they became very big.

"The mid '50s into the '60s — that was the best time." Here Marvin Scott (second from right) and friends at the Concord (1963).

AL ALTIERI: Latin music gives a girl a chance to undulate, to move more than anything else. You'd see a smartly dressed woman dancing the cha-cha or the meringue or the mambo, and you'd see something very sensuous.

Machito, whose real name was Frank Grillo, was at the Concord together with his sister Graciella, a world-famous Latin singer. Everyone came to see them. They could bring out the rhythms in anybody.

One night I was backstage waiting to go on with the big band, and Machito was on stage playing a wild mambo. A young, very scantily clad lady was singing, and her bosom kept bouncing out of her dress. Naturally, I and the other musicians were watching from the wings. Then, just behind me, I heard someone say "Marrone!" I turned. It was Mitzi Gaynor. She was also waiting to go on to do her act and watching from the wings. The rhythm was so good that I turned around and began dancing with her backstage. Afterwards, I said to the other musicians, "Don't touch me. I just danced with Mitzi Gaynor."

Machito, Perez Prado, Tito Puente, Sonny Rossi, they were all here. Sonny always befriended a younger girl. We called him the baby stealer. The musicians all wore rumba shirts. I owned a blue one with big ruffled sleeves.

ELAINE MARKSON: The hotels all had their dance teams with fancy names like Florenzio and Isabella. The man was usually Italian, never Jewish.

JACKIE HORNER: I had been a professional dancer and worked all over the country and South America, and I did a stint as a Rockette. Then in 1953, a dancer friend of mine invited me up to the Catskills, and that's how I became a "mambonik" working for Tony and Lucille Colon, who ran the dance concession at Grossinger's.

Latin was all the craze. Rumba had come in during the '40s and was still going strong, but everyone wanted mambo and cha-cha. Meringue and bossa nova came in a little bit later, around 1963. All of us could do the routines that Patrick Swayze and Jennifer Grey did in *Dirty Dancing*. In fact, I used to bring the watermelon plugged with vodka to our staff parties just like in the movie.

Tony and Lucille had come to Grossinger's from the Concord in 1947. Tony was born in Spain, and Lucille—a tiny little woman—was

A Champagne Hour production number at Grossinger's in 1957.

French. During the week they ran a posh dance studio in Manhattan, and on weekends they taught at Grossinger's.

Every hotel, big or small, had a resident dance team. There were Stella and José, very big on tango, at Stevensville. Mike Terace and Nilda were at Kutsher's. Esther Manor, Avon Lodge, Chester's, Swan Lake, and the President all had their dancers. But the Concord and Grossinger's had the biggest staffs. At Grossinger's we had ten teachers from Memorial Day to Labor Day.

Here's what a dance teacher's schedule was like. At 9:30 we

started teaching, and we kept going until six o'clock, when we'd break for dinner. At seven, on a full stomach, we'd go right into dance rehearsal. At nine, we'd change into costumes for our ten o'clock show. Then we'd dance with our pupils from eleven to one. And after all that, we'd head out for Mambo Night at some restaurant or club in the area.

Dancers don't eat that much during the day, but we'd eat like crazy at two in the morning. Most of the time we went to Corey's Chinese Restaurant in Liberty, the big after-hours place. Everyone fell in there about 1:30 A.M. People came from all the hotels, but tables were set up only for the Grossinger and Concord teachers. Everybody else had to shift for themselves. Guests from the hotels came, too. They couldn't wait to watch the dancers get up and do their stuff. One couple might do a special samba. Another pair would do a complicated tango. Sometimes threesomes like Cuban Pete, Millie, and Marilyn would perform. It was a time of release for all the dancers and a chance to showcase what we could do.

We'd dance till four, five o'clock in the morning. But come nine, we were up again and ready for another day's work. This went on around the clock.

At Grossinger's, we taught dancing in a studio similar to the one in *Dirty Dancing*. There were five mirrored rooms and a good floor. At first we danced to 78s, then 45s, then tapes. The charge was six half-hour lessons for $35. I got $2 a lesson; the rest went to Tony and Lucille, who turned over 15 percent of it to Grossinger's. It was a gold mine. I made maybe $20 a day and worked my tuchis off, but I loved it.

Every so often I'd be giving a lesson, and Milton Blackstone would come by.

"What are you teaching that guy?" he'd ask.

"Mambo."

"Don't let him get too close to you," he'd say.

At first we lived three in a room, but later we each got a room of our own with a private bath. We had lots of closet space, which we needed for all our costumes and crinolines. Our outfits reflected the glamour of the times. We'd change three or four times a day.

Since many of our guests were in the "rag business," all the dancers were treated to terrific buys on clothes. We'd go to the garment center in Manhattan and get designer stuff wholesale. Our clothes were as glamorous as any of the guests'.

The biggest showcase was the nightclub at Grossinger's. It was very intimate with two terraced floors. We called the lower level the pits, and the upper level was the graveyard.

It was mambo time — a glamorous, glittering era.

LOU GOLDSTEIN: There was a long entrance to the nightclub called the gangplank. All the single people would sit and look the field over as guys and girls walked through the gangplank into the nightclub. What was especially interesting were the fat little guys with the big stomachs. They'd come down the gangplank, and it seemed like they could hardly walk. Then the Latin music would start, and all of a sudden, they'd come to life. They'd run to their instructors, start dancing, and somehow they would become taller and sleeker as they moved to the music.

But the minute the music stopped, an amazing transformation would take place. They'd become short and fat again, looking like they could hardly walk.

JACKIE HORNER: Friday nights at Grossinger's was Champagne Hour. This was a contest everyone wanted to be in, a chance to shine and show off what they could do. But only five men and five women, not married to each other, would be selected as contestants. Each one was paired with an instructor and got out on the dance floor before God and everyone else. Most of the time, they were very good dancers. A lot of people stayed the entire summer, and they lived to dance. Very seldom would you see a shlep in Champagne Hour.

There would be three judges who sat apart from each other in different areas of the stage. Linda Darnell, Jayne Mansfield, Charlton Heston, John Garfield, Shelley Winters, George Abbott, Doris Day—these were some of the Champagne Hour judges.

The show would open with a production number danced by the ten teachers: a lindy or peabody, a meringue or cha-cha. Then two couples, each comprised of a guest and teacher, danced something of their choice. The band picked the songs—numbers like "Miami Beach Rumba" or "Green Eyes" or "The Peanut Vendor." After the first two couples performed, there'd be another production number, and then two more couples would compete.

After each couple had performed, all the contestants would be called back to do about eight bars. It was kind of like an encore and a chance for the judges and audience to refresh their minds. While the judges voted, a final production number was performed. Then the winners were announced. One man and one woman were selected as King and Queen of the Champagne Hour, and Tony and Lucille presented them with a bottle of champagne and gorgeous trophies.

Then there were the bungalow bunnies that you saw in *Dirty Dancing.* They were in the hotel all week long, but they stayed in outlying buildings where it was nice and private. The husbands only

The hotels all had resident dance instructors. The gentleman here taught the ladies to dance at Schenk's Paramount, 1953.

Competing for the bottle of champagne: Marvin Scott and dance instructor.

came up on weekends, so it was party time for them Monday through Friday. They took dance lessons from the male instructors during the day. At night, after the show, the male instructors came back to dance with the pupils. They kept themselves busy around the clock.

MARVIN SCOTT: You'd see a change in these women on Sunday afternoons when the husbands went back to the city, leaving them for the week. Suddenly, they became swingers. They were looking for the young guys, and they became hip. But come Friday night, the husbands would come up and they'd turn back into nice, doting lovely housewives once again.

One woman in particular stands out. She came up on a Friday afternoon with her husband and a kid about six years old. The husband went inside to check in, and the kid started yelling, "Mommy, Mommy, can I have money for the pinball machine?"

She turned to her child. "Here, go play. But stop calling me Mommy."

JACKIE HORNER: There were the Johnnys like in *Dirty Dancing.* One dance teacher on our staff would make out while Champagne Hour was going on, knock off a girl, come back and do the rest of the show.

"Where the hell were you?" I'd ask when he'd rush in to dance with me.

"See that little redhead in the fourth row?" he'd say, and he'd smile.

But in spite of the bungalow bunnies and the Johnnys, I think of it as an innocent time. They didn't represent the rule. I worked for Tony and Lucille until they left in 1973. Then I took over the dance concession and ran it until the hotel closed. By then, things had changed. For one thing, relationships were no longer so innocent. Of course, as I said, things had happened before, but not so often and not so suddenly. You acted with more respect for one another. There always was liquor and probably more drinks were poured in one night for a teacher than anyone else, but if we drank two of them, that was a lot. Girls never got into bed with someone they didn't know at least three months—and then in hopes of getting married. It was mambo time, and it was also a more innocent time. And that in itself was wonderful.

FIVE

ONLY
AT THE CONCORD

JOEY GREENWALD: In 1911, my grandfather Abraham Greenwald brought his wife's cousin and her husband, Arthur Winarick, to the United States from Russia. The two men opened a barber shop in New York City, and Arthur Winarick invented a hair tonic in the basement of that barber shop. He asked my grandfather whether he wanted to put in $100 and become a partner. "Who's going to buy that crap?" my grandfather said. "For $100 I can feed my family."

My grandfather went on to become a founder of the barber's union, and Arthur Winarick worked on his product, which he named Jeris

Hair Tonic. He expanded quickly into the barber supply business and built Jeris into a multimillion-dollar concern.

MILTON KUTSHER: In the summer of 1932, Arthur Winarick and his wife were vacationing at the Ideal House, a boarding-house in Kiamesha Lake. As in a lot of other cases at the time, the owner was having trouble making a go of it, and Winarick gave her a small mortgage. By 1935, he'd picked up the hotel itself.

PAUL GROSSINGER: As the story goes, Arthur Winarick came to Grossinger's when we had a full house. He couldn't get a room, so he said, "I'm going to get even with you and build my own hotel." And he built the Concord.

DAVE LEVINSON: Arthur Winarick used to say, "I'm gonna build. I'm gonna be cheaper than all you guys. I'm gonna take all your business away." His vision was to be big enough to take in all the business in the Catskills and leave everybody starve. That's what he would talk about all the time. He realized, even back then, that a hotel should be one building, one plant, while I was still trying to copy "single-mingle" hotels with cabins in the woods. He gave the Catskills a big push.

IRVING COHEN: In 1936, he acquired a Kiamesha property from two brothers whom he lent money to build a swimming pool. This place was called the Concord Plaza. In 1939, he incorporated the properties as the Concord Hotel. I began working for the Concord then.

At that time it was next to impossible to get a job in New York City. I was ready to do anything, anywhere. So I went to the Jupiter Agency on 62nd and Third Avenue, where they booked all the help for Sullivan County. They got me a job at Grossinger's as a busboy, and later I became a waiter. On my station I had John Garfield, Milton Berle, Moss Hart, Irving Berlin, and Eddie Cantor.

I worked with a man named Sam Miner, who had originally managed Ratner's restaurant on Delancey Street. He was hired by Arthur Winarick to be in charge of the kitchen and dining room at his new hotel, and he took me with him. We were the first ones to come. He bought the equipment and tables and set up the kitchen and the dining room.

The place was nothing when we got there, just a blank at the start. It was a little hotel with about thirty people. Mrs. Winarick took care of the drapes. I drove her to New York to buy material, and she sewed them herself. I was single and I really loved the Winaricks. They were like my parents.

GORDON WINARICK: In 1935, I started out as a kid amongst the crowd. The adults would sit, visit, and talk. They would acquire, build, and develop. The Concord was the extension of my Uncle Arthur's dream. He came out of Russia with visions of the palatial buildings of the upper class. Everybody aspired to live in a palace, and he fashioned all the huge buildings at the Concord to meet that dream.

From the start the Concord had a different look. Where all the other hotels were made of wood, he said, "I'll make my hotel timeless, out of concrete and steel. My heirs can always make the modifications."

Before the buildings of the 1939 World's Fair were demolished, he bought a lot of things from that site. He bought steel structures

Big and elaborate even back then: an aerial view of the Concord, 1939.

in their entirety. At one point, he even envisioned transporting whole buildings up here.

IRVING COHEN: During the war we couldn't get steel to build a new dining room. Winarick heard a 125th Street ferryboat was for sale. He bought it, dismantled it, and used the steel for the Concord dining room. Winarick hired the designer of the Copacabana and the Latin Quarter to do the job.

GORDON WINARICK: One of my first assignments was to study formal gardens. I spent days in the library reading, researching. The Concord was only a resort, but Winarick wanted to get the feel of a palace. At one time we had close to 50,000 tulips on the approachway to the hotel.

　　Winarick was kind but relentless in getting things done. He was a man of guts, figures, and instinct, and he got right to the point in everything. The formalities of life meant little to him, and he could not sit around for hours at a social meeting. He had an endless ability to absorb things. If there was a special core in your knowledge bank, he'd get it, make it part of him. People thought he was talking non-sense when he said he'd build an eleven-story building with an elevator, but he did it. Some of the other hotel owners in the area admired him. Many didn't.

MILTON KUTSHER: Since Winarick was a man of means, he built that hotel without having to borrow two cents. He lived and breathed the hotel business, and he talked hotels all the time. He'd come over to you on the street in Monticello and ask, "What are you paying for meat? What are you paying for eggs?"

GORDON WINARICK: There was a sense of the theatrical in him. "Mr. Weiss," he'd say, "when you come up to the hotel, I'll give you a brand-new room. What color do you like? You like it blue? I'll make it blue. The mattress—soft or hard? Soft? It'll be soft." The guy came up with his family, and in the room that was painted blue for him, they were unwrapping the furniture and laying out the soft mattress. Talk about theatrics.

　　My uncle's philosophy was "We treat everyone like a king or queen here. Anything they say, it's yes, yes, yes. If a guest wants his sheets changed twice a day, we'll do it. If a guest wants breakfast in bed, he'll have it. We don't say no to anything. At the Concord, it's living luxuriously."

ROBERT PARKER: My grandfather kept three sets of furniture in the basement. If someone checked in and didn't like the furniture, he'd replace it with a set from the basement. Then he sent the original furniture out to be refinished and put back for other guests. The whole thing cost him maybe $100. People thought he was extravagant, but do you know what that's worth in PR? People believed there was nothing he wouldn't do for his customers.

ROBERT TOWERS: Winarick believed in grand dining rooms, great entertainment, big rooms, suites with two bathrooms. That was revolutionary for the Catskills. He was driven by an ambition such as few people have—a real empire builder. He was determined to run the biggest hotel in the world.

IRVING COHEN: In 1943, the Concord opened year-round. Sam Miner didn't want to stay through the winter and neither did his wife, so I succeeded him as maitre d'. We had no business that year, but we used to call Grossinger's, and when they were filled up, we knew we were going to get busy for the weekend. That's how we knew how much to order. It was rough competition for a few years, but Winarick developed his own clientele.

He never degraded anybody. As a matter of fact, he built people up. If guests knocked somebody on the staff, he would not go for it.

"I have the best people working for me," he would say. "We don't have any second-rate people." He would point out problems to the staff, but he would never yell or harass you. If you weren't good, he just got rid of you.

He consulted everybody. He used to sit with the chambermaids and go over a set of plans—like they knew what they were looking at—and show them a building he was putting up.

"What do you think of the bathroom?" he would ask. "Do you think this is a good place for beds to go in this room?"

ROBERT PARKER: The man never graduated from high school; he was totally self-educated. Yet he could carry on a conversation about

Arthur Winarick, founder of the Concord (left), with newspaper columnist and television personality Ed Sullivan.

fragrances, music, medicine, business. He was provincial and worldly at the same time. Every time I met with him, I learned something.

CEIL BECKMAN JACOBS: What he didn't know, he learned, he studied. His mind was an open book. He couldn't speak the King's English, but he made sure you knew what he meant.

JOEY GREENWALD: Dressed in the same pants he wore when he worked in the Jeris factory, Arthur Winarick would be stopped at the gate. Sometimes his own employees didn't know him.

BILLY ECKSTINE: Sometimes his own guests didn't know him. If the joint was crowded and people were checking in, he'd grab some luggage and walk in there with it like one of the bellboys. He grabbed a guest's bag once to help clear the lobby out, and when he got out to the car, the guy wanted to tip him.

IRVING COHEN: He would walk around with the dirty pants and the white shirt with the suspenders and the hat with the filthy band. He never carried money.

Later on, he divided his two businesses, the hotel and Jeris, equally between his children, Clara and Julie. Clara and her husband, Ray Parker, were interested in the hotel, while Julie wanted to run Jeris.

One day Julie called Mr. Winarick and told him he wanted to buy a company in Pittsburgh named Dr. Ellis. They made a green, mucky hair lotion. "If you want to buy it," the old man said, "bring the people up here and we'll find out what they want for it."

Julie walked into the dining room with the president, accountant, and attorney for Dr. Ellis. The family table was near the desk—you can hear conversations going on. They had lunch, and then Julie says, "Irving, get my father."

At that time, they were constructing a building. The old man came in soaking wet, wearing dirty shoes. He loved construction. "How are you, Sonny?" he said. That was what he always called Julie. Then he sits down at the table with the four of them.

The three men from Pittsburgh are looking at each other and thinking, "Who's this character?"

They talk for a while, and then the old man says to Julie, "Come to the price." Julie gives him a figure. "You're paying too much, Sonny," he says. "If you buy it, you're going to be doing it against my wishes."

Julie asks, "Why?"

The others ask, "Why?"

"Last year," the old man begins, "your income was X dollars and you lost X dollars. The year before your sales were X, and you lost X amount of money. Why should I buy a business that's losing money? Why should we give you this much money for such a business?"

They looked at him. "How do you know what our business is?"

He said, "I know. Otherwise, why would I talk to you?"

After they left, he said, "Look, Sonny, this business is worth X dollars. If you pay more, you're not gonna make money on it."

He got it for his price. A few days later I was driving Mr. Winarick to New York City, and I said, "I don't like to eavesdrop, but you were sitting right next to me in the dining room. How did you happen to know how much business they did?"

He told me, "I have this banker friend who I do business with so I asked him to look into that company. He told me everything. That's how I do things. I make it my business to find out."

CEIL BECKMAN JACOBS: Arthur Winarick was an old-time viola player and loved concerts. In 1940, he brought in Alexander Olshanetsky, who had composed many musicals for the Yiddish theater. He was the first bandleader at the Concord. During the '40s, there was an orchestra of thirty-five to forty musicians that played Rachmaninoff, Beethoven, Tchaikovsky. There were concerts at least once a week.

GLORIA WINARICK: In 1945, Sholom Secunda succeeded Olshanetsky, and he was there until 1963. I knew Secunda since I was a child. He worked in the Yiddish theater with my father.

CEIL BECKMAN JACOBS: Sholom became very famous in the late 1930s with his song "Bei Mer Bist du Schön." Eddie Cantor had the chance to record it, but he turned it down because he thought it was too Yiddish. Other singers did the same. Then these three Greek girls had a go at it, and it became a big hit. They were, of course, the Andrews Sisters.

AL ALTIERI: One time Sholom decided to do something special with Tchaikovsky's *1812 Overture*. He arranged for the security guards to shoot blanks in their pistols in order to simulate the cannon shots in the piece. But he didn't tell anyone in the orchestra, so the musicians didn't know what was going to happen. I was playing timpani and sitting in the back of the orchestra. I saw these gentlemen on the sidelines raise their guns in the air, ready to shoot. Then the guns went off. The cello players dropped their bows. Everybody spun around. The entire orchestra stopped. A lady in the front row got up with her fur coat and started to run. It was like a train wreck.

IRVING COHEN: At the start we had no indoor nightclub, just the Rio Bamba outside the main building about where the tennis courts are now. Mr. Winarick also bought a series of smaller hotels that were close by. We had outbuildings because the main building couldn't accommodate all the guests. Then he bought a hotel across the road called Gluck's Hillside, up on the mountain—a beautiful place.

GLORIA WINARICK: By 1946, the Concord was an eighty-eight–room hotel, and the weekly rate was $77.50. There was a large nucleus of almost 300 season guests, and the atmosphere was very elegant. On

Friday and Saturday nights, the men wore black tie, and the women wore evening gowns with white gloves. At five o'clock the women would go to the vault to take out their jewelry. There were some magnificent pieces. Guests would go into the dining room to see what Mrs. So-and-So was wearing that evening. In February you'd start to think, "Hmm, there are eight Saturday nights for the summer season. I better start buying my evening gowns now." It was the postwar period, and a lot of people had money.

ROBERT MERRILL: By the 1950s the Concord was starting to outstrip Grossinger's, which was a little frugal when it came to paying. They felt that if you played Grossinger's you didn't have to take all the money. The Concord paid decent money, and it didn't bargain. They began getting better acts.

GORDON WINARICK: Always big names, top people. Buster Crabbe, the Olympic swimming champion who played Tarzan in the movies

Buster Crabbe surrounded by a group of young admirers in the Concord pool.

was the swimming pro. (Grossinger's countered with Florence Chadwick, the woman who conquered the English Channel.) Jimmy Demaret was the golf pro. Ray Parker saw a guy diving off the cliffs in Acapulco, and he brought him here to dive into the pool. A couple of times a day people would assemble around the pool. It was like watching Old Faithful at Yellowstone.

MIKE STRAUSS: They say Arthur Winarick wondered how big a golf course Grossinger's had. Eighteen, he was told. "Then we'll have forty-five." The nine-hole Challenger came first, then the eighteen-hole International, then in 1962, the 7,672-yard Monster championship course.

GORDON WINARICK: Grossinger's was established, and it had one style. We were newer and had another style. We were on two different tracks. Grossinger's had knotty pine: tradition. We had terazzo: upbeat. Grossinger's was more sedate, more establishment-oriented. We had the shakers and the movers, the upscale, younger people.

GLORIA WINARICK: Sarah Churchill was here. People from film, theater, letters, politics. You sat in the nightclub, and at the next table was Robert Goulet, Vincent Impellitteri who was mayor of New York City, Lucille Ball and her husband Gary Morton. Celebrities would

Celebrities, like Gary Morton and Lucille Ball, were always part of the crowd in the Concord nightclub.

autograph menus, pose for pictures with guests, do impromptu entertaining in the Night Owl Lounge. The ads in the *New York Times* said "Hotels—like people—are judged by the company they keep." And Philly Greenwald was responsible for it all.

JOEY GREENWALD: My grandfather never took Arthur Winarick up on his offer to invest in Jeris, but all three of his sons became involved in the Concord. My father, Phil Greenwald, is the one who really became identified with the hotel. In 1935, when he was seventeen, he worked weekends as a lifeguard, and then he became a cashier.

My father began hanging out with the talent bookers Beckman and Pransky in the '40s. He got to know everyone around the Broadway beat. In the '50s, he took over as exclusive talent booker for the Concord, and right away he went all out for the big names.

ERROL DANTE: When Philly first got the job in 1955 booking the Concord, he pulled quite a coup. Tony Martin was the number one singing star in America, and Milton Berle was Mr. Television. Philly went to Berle and asked, "You want to play the Concord?"

And Berle said, "Who do you have?"

"I have Tony Martin."

Then he went to Tony Martin. "Do you want to play the Concord?"

And Martin said, "Who do you have?"

"I have Milton Berle."

He got them both.

TONY MARTIN: I had heard about the Mountains from entertainers who'd been there, people like Harry Richman and George Jessel who told me it was the place to go. They used to go up there to break things in. I wasn't breaking in then since I was a known performer. Still, I was hyped to come to the Concord.

The Winaricks took a liking to me, and I played there many times. They would sit up close to the stage, and I would sing love songs like "Fascination" to Mrs. Winarick. Mr. Winarick could take or leave the comedians, but he loved singers.

ERROL DANTE: After getting Berle and Martin, Philly went after and personally brought out some of the greatest stars, performers like Judy Garland, Marlene Dietrich, Maurice Chevalier.

Philly took out a full-page ad for Chevalier in the Paris edition of the *New York Times* when he appeared at the Concord. Chevalier told Philly that never in his whole career had anyone ever taken out a full-page ad for him.

JOEY GREENWALD: Sometimes at the Monticello Racetrack my father would see a performer losing some money. Right on the spot he'd make a deal—lend some money and have an act at a bargain rate. He also used to get Broadway stars on their night off; Yul Brynner came up while he was appearing in *The King and I*. He sat cross-legged on the stage and sang what I think were Russian folk songs.

ERROL DANTE: Erskine Hawkins, the jazz trumpet player, was playing in the lounge. A young woman was sitting there. Philly told Erskine, "Introduce her, get her up to sing."

Ernie said, "Ladies and Gentlemen, Miss Lisa Magnolia!" It was Liza Minnelli.

And when bandleader Marty Beck introduced Maurice Chevalier, he said, "Ladies and Gentlemen, Maurice Chevrolet!"

JOEY GREENWALD: Getting Sophie Tucker, Joe E. Lewis, and Harry Richman to perform on one bill was what my father considered his greatest coup. "The others brag about getting one star," he said. "I got three." The only problem was deciding how to place them. He was dealing with three big egos. Finally they agreed on the arrangement: Joe E. Lewis opened and Harry Richman closed. Sophie Tucker went in the middle.

Once my father got a call from the William Morris agency. They told him they had a country and western singer he could have for $50.

"Country and western," my father said, "I wouldn't have that in my hotel for anything in the world, no matter the price."

"But he's good."

"Good for him," my father said. "I wish him luck but I'll pass. What's his name anyway?"

"Elvis Presley."

He didn't pass on Woody Allen, but Woody didn't go over well at the Concord. Years later he returned as a guest with Diane Keaton.

The debonair Maurice Chevalier
peeks out from behind his Imperial
Room poster at the Concord, 1966.

Three on one bill: Philly Greenwald
(left) poses with a trio of stars he
brought to the Concord: (from left to
right) Harry Richman, Sophie Tucker,
and George Jessel.

MAURICE CHEVALIER

My father remembered that Woody liked malteds so he sent me to the coffee shop. I had to get a tray of malteds in nineteen different flavors.

My father introduced knockers at the Concord. They were sticks with a wooden ball at the end, and there'd be hundreds of them on the tables in the Imperial Room. Some people said the knockers were there because people were so full after dinner that they were too tired to applaud. But it was really because the room, seating 3,000, was so large that knockers carried the sound better.

The knockers remind me of Engelbert Humperdinck. When he came into his dressing room and saw the green walls, he complained that he couldn't work out of a green room. We repainted it for him, and he did a wonderful show.

Afterward, he complained that he couldn't understand why the

Taking it easy at the Concord around 1949. From left to right — standing: Alan "Blackie" Schackner, bandleader Marty Beck; seated: unidentified guest, talent booker Philly Greenwald, director of activities Mac Kinsbrunner.

crowd didn't like him. That's when we found out that in England people knock when they don't like an act. As much as we tried to explain, he wouldn't hear it. He never worked the Concord again.

GLORIA WINARICK: Philly gave a lot of performers a break even if he knew they weren't that good. He would throw them in on a Tuesday night, a Wednesday night. He could be tough as hell, but tell him a sad story and he'd be the first one with his hands in his pockets.

JOEY GREENWALD: My father loved the acts who were just starting out. Barbra Streisand would appear and he'd be just vaguely interested. But if an unknown juggler came on, he'd stop everything to watch him and leave when the headliner appeared.

ERROL DANTE: Greenwald had a great sense of promotion, a press agent's mind. When he was still single, Bess Myerson became the first Jewish Miss America. He got Walter Winchell to put in his column "Phil Greenwald and Bess Myerson are a four-alarm blaze."

They had never met each other. She called up the Concord. "How dare they say that?"

Philly had a retraction put in: "Phil Greenwald and Bess Myerson are *not* a four-alarm blaze."

He was friends with a lot of the great newspaper columnists like Ed Sullivan and Walter Winchell. Once Winchell wrote: "Phil Greenwald: Prop. of Concord." Philly explained to Arthur Winarick it meant "Phil Greenwald: Propagandist of the Concord."

GLORIA WINARICK: During the '40s and '50s Phil put out a weekly newspaper called the *Concord Evening News*. It was distributed to all guests and mailed to all former guests, had a calendar of events and all kinds of little gossipy items. People loved seeing their names in print. There'd be a photo with the caption "Dr. and Mrs. Stanley Berger checking in for another summer." The most ridiculous stories, invented by Philly of course, were about who was seen with whom, like "Mrs. and Mrs. Jerry Abrams are vacationing at the Concord along with Perry Como and his family."

"He did it!" Jimmy Durante lays the blame on Concord founder Arthur Winarick.

Philly Greenwald became exclusive talent booker for the Concord in the 1950s, and right away he went all out for the big names.

ERROL DANTE: Phil Greenwald was the greatest offstage performer, uniquely funny. He created a persona for himself. It was always: "What's the latest Philly Greenwald story?"

There are so many Philly Greenwald stories: the Tabasco in your Scotch, the salt in your coffee. Once Philly was in Puerto Rico with Allen and Rossi at the El San Juan Hotel. They had breakfast, lunch, dinner together. Philly would sign all the checks. "Oh no," he'd say, "you can't pick up a check. I love you guys."

Philly signs all the checks. Philly checks out a day ahead of time. Allen and Rossi go to the desk. They've got a bill for $6,800. They take a look at the checks: Philly had been signing "Allen and Rossi."

JOEY GREENWALD: Pat Henry was appearing once when he got an offer from Frank Sinatra to open for him in Palm Springs; it proved to be Pat's first big break.

"We're so proud of you," my father told him. "It's great news. I'll take care of everything. I'll book your flight and have you taken to the airport in style."

"Gee, thanks, Phil," Pat said. "It's wonderful. I really appreciate all you're doing for me."

"Don't even mention it," my father said. "Nothing is too good for a friend like you."

Pat left the Concord in a limo. While he was on his way to Kennedy Airport, my father called up JFK security. "Hello," my father said, "this is Pat Henry. I've been mugged. Some guy took my ID, credit cards, and my tickets for a flight to L.A. Please apprehend him at the gate." And they did.

TONY MARTIN: Philly Greenwald came over to me one day and said, "Hey, Tony, you going home? What can I buy you? What can I give you?"

I said, "Give me a nice little dog."

He gave me a Saint Bernard pup. Now I didn't want a Saint Bernard. We don't use Saint Bernards in California.

I named the dog Gypsy and got a box to keep it in, and went off to Chicago to work. I was there for two weeks. By the time I left town, I had to buy a new box for the dog—it had grown so much. Every place I went the dog kept growing, and I kept buying new boxes. I ended up spending $500 on boxes.

JERRY VALE: Phil Greenwald gave me my original booking at the Concord. Once he came into my dressing room and poured out a batch of children's shoes onto the floor.

"I don't want to embarrass you," he said, "but I know kids always need shoes. My family is in the shoe business. Take whatever you want."

I didn't want to embarrass him, so I knelt down and began picking out shoes. Phil kept saying, "Go ahead, go ahead, take whatever you want."

I picked out about five or six shoes and then started looking for the mates. It took me a while, looking around on my hands and knees, before I realized they were all for the left foot.

ERROL DANTE: Philly was larger than life. When he died in 1982, I was more affected than when anyone except my own parents died. To this day, they still talk about Phil Greenwald at the Friars Club.

STEVE ROSSI: Soon after I teamed up with Marty Allen, Greenwald saw our act and booked us at the Concord.

A black-tie gathering at the Concord. From left to right: Cary Grant, unidentified man, Milton Berle, Errol Dante.

Our first day up in the Mountains, we appeared in one of the smaller rooms. A big blizzard was under way, and only about 100 people were in the audience. We went out, and we couldn't buy a laugh. But one person in front was laughing her head off. When the show was over, Marty and I were sitting—hiding, actually—in the back lobby, we were so embarrassed. We get a page from one of the bellboys. "Miss Trydelle would like to see you at the front desk."

Standing there behind the counter was the one and only person who had laughed at our show that night. "Boys," she said in a beautiful French accent, "you wair so funnee. I nevair laugh so much in my life.

"I am zee reservations manager," she continued while Marty and I stood there dumbfounded, "and I invite you to be my guests here."

MARTY ALLEN: Lorraine "Frenchie" Trydelle, I learned later, started as a telephone operator and then took over the switchboard. Soon after, old man Winarick picked her to be reservations and general manager, and she ran the whole place. It was her idea to have suites with two baths, to go after conventions and corporations. She was a major domo, a dynamo, brilliant and beautiful.

Soon after our debut in that outer room, Phil invited me to have lunch with him and Frenchie.

"You're a Parisienne," I said to her. "Are you interested in Rodin?"

"Did Philly tell you to ask that?" She thought Philly set it up, that this was another one of his practical jokes. "Do you know who Rodin is?"

"Yeah," I said, "I know who Rodin is. He's not an agent. He's a great artist, and I have a batch of his pictures with me. Would it sound crazy if I told you they're in my room and I can show them to you?"

"Bring zem to my office."

"No. I'll leave the door open, but you'll have to come to my room."

We compromised; she came to the door of my room, and I brought my pictures out into the hall.

In April 1960, the old man Winarick, who loved Frenchie so much, threw the wedding for us in the Imperial Room. There were 3,500 guests, and Perry Como's wife was her matron of honor. We were married on stage, and the cantor was Richard Tucker.

They gave us a penthouse on top of the Towers—one of the buildings at the Concord. That's where we lived. And Steve had a suite.

Jack Benny and Sammy Davis, Jr. on the Concord golf course.

In Greenwald's corner (from left to right): Philly Greenwald, columnist Earl Wilson, and Nipsey Russell.

Our marriage lasted almost sixteen years. Then she died of cancer. When we have a tragedy in life, the only healer is time. I didn't work for a while. Then I got started again. I knew that's what Frenchie would have wanted. Still I couldn't bring myself to perform in the Mountains for quite a while. A lot of things came apart.

STEVE ROSSI: Marty and I broke up our act around 1972, and got back together in 1979, and we started over by coming back to the Catskills. We probably have headlined at the Concord more than any other team in history, maybe because it was our home. The Concord made us professionals. From there we were able to go anywhere.

NIPSEY RUSSELL: I was born in Atlanta and did some of my growing-up in Harlem. I had done only local entertaining and was playing the Baby Grand on 125th Street and Lenox Avenue when Billy Eckstine introduced me to Philly Greenwald, sometime in the '50s. Philly booked me into the big room, and I opened for Billy Eckstine.

When I headlined at the Concord, it was like a black entertainer scoring at the Apollo, a classical pianist performing at Carnegie Hall, an actor winning the Academy Award. Once you scored at the Concord, you were set. Everyone wanted you.

JERRY VALE: I got booked at the Concord around 1957 or 1958, and that appearance got the attention of a lot of people. In those days, when you said "Just Closed at the Concord" it was a great advertisement, like saying "Just Closed at the Copacabana in New York City."

ERROL DANTE: Judy made her comeback at the Concord in 1961 after not working for a long time. It was just before her Carnegie Hall concert. To give you an idea of how prices have skyrocketed, she got $7,000 for that performance and it was considered unbelievable. Nobody had ever gotten that much before. Today a headliner gets $75,000 to $100,000.

Judy came up on a Sunday night. People usually check out Sunday mornings, but they stayed to see her.

GLORIA WINARICK: The night she went on was one of the most exciting ever in the Catskills. People were standing on their chairs. At the end of the show Judy brought Liza on stage. Liza was still a kid then, and the two of them did a number together. While they were dancing, Liza's hair kept falling in her face, and Judy kept pushing it back. It was the simplest and sweetest motherly gesture.

ROBERT TOWERS: Streisand came up on a Friday night before she made *Funny Girl*. The William Morris Agency said, "Look, you're getting her for $500. Later on you won't be able to buy her for anything."

She came up—a little girl in a gunnysack dress with a big voice. She tore the place apart.

GLORIA WINARICK: For about nine summers an act called Hines, Hines, and Dad played the Night Owl Lounge.

JOHNNY PRANSKY: I can still remember the day these three black guys came into our office in the Woodstock Hotel on 43rd Street in Manhattan. I was really booked up and didn't want to listen, but before I knew it, the older guy—who was the other guys' father—was setting up drums in front of my desk, and the two younger ones were tap dancing away. They were great! I booked them into the Lounge at the Concord.

GLORIA WINARICK: Gregory Hines, Maurice Hines, their dad Chink —a heavyset jovial guy, an absolute angel—and their mother lived up at the Concord those nine summers. The men were brilliant talents, and also they were very friendly. They'd hang around with the guests during the day, play ball with them.

ROBERT KOLE: Maurice and Gregory were wonderful guys, but dirty basketball players. They'd grab my shirt every time I'd try to move with the ball. They sang, danced, did everything, used all those years to sharpen their talent. For a while they teamed up with one of the greatest tap dancers ever, Bunny Briggs.

BILLY ECKSTINE: I've heard it said that I was the first black headliner in the Catskills. I first appeared there in 1949. I don't want to sound naive, but that was something I was never aware of. I don't remember breaking down walls—there were no walls to break down.

Billy Eckstine teeing off at the Concord's Monster golf course and (inset) taking a break with Steve Lawrence and Eydie Gorme.

NIPSEY RUSSELL: Various black performers played the Catskills through the years. Bill "Bojangles" Robinson had appeared at Grossinger's years before. I was told Avon Long, one of the first to play Sporting Life, had been all over the Catskills doing songs from *Porgy and Bess*. But when I came on the scene, aside from Billy Eckstine and Lena Horne, black performers were variety entertainers, not headliners. And stars like Billy and Lena headlined anywhere, even though in some places they may have had to sleep on the beach.

People say timing is everything. I went on to headline. It was around the time of social integration, and I was accepted. After my first appearance at the Concord, I played it five or six times a year. I must have played it hundreds of times.

They had college intersession weekends back then. The kids who came up were politically aware. I'd do my act, and afterwards in the coffee shop, or in the lobby, or sitting with some group in a room, we'd have some pretty heavy discussions. I learned from these kids, and they learned from me.

A study in 1950s modernism: the entrance lobby of the Concord and grand stairway to the upper lounge.

IRVING COHEN: My most exciting time was in the '60s. We had so many season guests: the garment center people, the furriers, the people from the hat district. Many of them were foreigners. Today most of them have sold out to big companies and live in Florida. Every once in a while they come for the High Holy Days with their families to show them where they spent their time and also to show them a little bit of Jewish life.

We had Sam Lefrak's parents for many summers. They were lovely people. They couldn't speak English, just Yiddish and Polish. I became pretty friendly with the old man. I would ask him how he was doing. Always, I got the same answer:

"Irving, ez geyt mir git." [I'm doing well.] "Ick hob gekoyft nokh a hoyzele." In other words he bought another little house. Little did I realize.

"Sam," I said, "why does your father need all these little hoyzelekh?"

"Irving, what he calls a hoyzele is a fifteen-story building on Long Island with five elevators."

Donald Trump's parents had a waitress named Helen who always took care of them. And I became friendly with the father, Fred Trump. We used to talk about our children, and he would say, "Irving, I'm a millionaire now"—he had a lot of property in Brooklyn—"but when my son Donald comes out of school, he's gonna make me a billionaire. That's how bright he is."

Perry Como grabs Ray Parker by the arm as he describes his confrontation with the Monster.

SHARON PARKER: One night walking around the dining room, I passed by an elderly couple. The man was wearing a suit of the most beautiful fabric.

"Sir," I said to him. "That's a magnificent suit."

"Do you really like it?" he asked modestly.

"I love it. Where did you get it?"

"My son made it for me."

"Who is your son?"

"Ralph Lauren."

NAOMI PARKER FRIEDMAN: In the early 1960s, my father got a phone call from someone who said an Indian maharajah was coming up. "Stop putting me on," he said and hung up the phone.

A few days later, the same phone call, the same message. This time a reservation was made, and a few days later, he arrived. Diamond-studded and with a complete entourage—the maharajah came to the Concord.

ROBERT PARKER: During the 1960s a guest from Oklahoma would walk around giving out $5 tips. You brought him a newspaper—$5 tip. You took a message for him—$5 tip.

One day he came over to me and asked me to cash a $1,000 check. In those days, that was a big check.

"Call my bank," he said.

I called up his bank. "Anything up to seven figures is okay," I was told. "He always keeps a minimum of seven figures in his account."

Who was he? Just another Oklahoma oilman.

ARTHUR RICHMAN: Handling sports forums at the Concord and Nevele, I've brought up people like Pete Rose, Joe DiMaggio, Tom Seaver, Willie Mays, Bob Gibson. Once we even managed to have George Steinbrenner at the Concord.

There was a terrible blizzard that day, and nobody thought he would show up. But lo and behold, in the midst of the storm, a car pulled up and out stepped George. Not only did he work the program, but he remained for a couple of hours and answered every question and signed every program that he was asked to.

IRVING RUDD: Back in 1976 Muhammad Ali was training at the Concord for a title defense. Our entourage took over all the rooms in the golf clubhouse. Ali even had his own cook, a Muslim woman named Lana Shabazz, who specialized in fresh fruits and vegetables and made a hell of a pecan pie.

Dick Gregory was great friends with Ali and was the house nutritionist. He had a room set up with juicing machines, oranges, grapefruits, health stuff. My mother-in-law, who was up there with us, loved to go into that room and try out his drinks. She developed a yen for them.

One day while Dick Gregory was off on one of his lecture gigs, my mother-in-law went into the nutrition room hoping to get something to drink. But she couldn't find anything and was disappointed. Later that night when Gregory returned she was waiting for him.

"Hey, where were you?" she asked. "I was looking for you all day."

"Why? What's the matter?" Dick said.

"All day I was looking for something good to drink."

With that Dick Gregory gave her a big hug. "Mama. Mama. I was busy all day."

"Okay," she said. "Okay, don't worry about it. You won't get in trouble. But maybe now you can get me a little something to drink?"

She didn't know anything about Dick Gregory. She thought the nutrition room came with the Concord territory.

Ali's bodyguards had a time with him because although training was strictly business at the Concord, Muhammad was always a free spirit. One Friday night, cold turkey, he shows up in the main dining room. Big as life, with that regal presence, all smiles, he walks through the room.

"Muhammad!" "Champ! Champ! Champ!"

Gray-haired old bubbes were calling out his name. They loved him, and he loved it. Ali bent down and kissed the old ladies, shook

Muhammad Ali sparring with Jimmy Ellis at the Concord.

hands with everybody. They all had themselves a time including his bodyguards—but that was on safe territory.

Another time Ali took off from his roadwork and wandered into South Fallsburg. It was like a scene out of *Rocky*. Kids trailed after him chanting "Ali! Ali!" People flocked around him asking for autographs. He was the Pied Piper in a sweat suit. The people loved every minute of him out there in the open, but his bodyguards sweated it out.

ROBERT TOWERS: After I left Grossinger's in the late 1940s, I was a partner in an advertising company with Milton Blackstone and some other men. Milton lost interest in the business and left. I saw it was going nowhere. I said to the others, "Gentlemen, whatever I created is mine, whatever you created is yours." I borrowed money from the late Ben Slutsky of the Nevele and opened my own shop in 1954. The Concord and the Nevele are two of my accounts.

After Isaac Bashevis Singer won the Nobel Prize for literature in 1978 and delivered that wonderful speech about the Yiddish language, I said to my secretary: "Look up I. B. Singer. He just may be in the phone directory."

There was a number listed. I dialed. I was shocked when a voice answered, "Hellooo."

"Mr. Singer," I said, "you have just won God knows how much money. But you don't have a receptionist or a secretary to answer your phone?"

"I like to answer the phone by myself," he said. "Sooo, what is it?"

"My name is Robert Towers. I represent the Concord Hotel. I have brought Chaim Weizmann to the Catskills, Abba Eban when his name was Aubrey Eban, Rabbi Stephen Wise . . ."

"I heard of the Concord. A beautiful place. Many, many years ago I used to stay in Woodbourne. In those days, I couldn't afford the Concord. So, what do you want me for?"

"Mr. Singer," I said, "I want you to deliver a lecture on the books you have written, on the malaise of our society . . ."

"Mr. Towers, let me interrupt you. If you were a community center, a Jewish organization, if you were a synagogue, a temple, I would come. But you're in business. The Concord makes a lot of money."

"It's a pleasure to talk to you," I said. Then I hung up.

I got an editor of the *Forward* on the phone, the late Simon Weber, a beautiful man. Weber had been Singer's editor for many years. "Look," I said, "I would like to have Mr. Singer for Passover week."

"So, what do you want from me?"

"I want you to appear on stage with him. You know his books, you know his columns, you know his readings."

"So, you don't think I'm worth at least half as much?"

"You've got it," I said.

And Isaac Bashevis Singer appeared with Simon Weber at the Concord.

I met Henry Kissinger on a plane coming back from Florida and invited him to appear at the Concord. "I'm running out of people," I confessed to him. "Herschel Bernardi—he's not around any more. Rabbi Stephen Wise has gone on to his heavenly reward. You would be a sensation."

Henry Kissinger signs autographs after his lecture at the Concord.

"Oh, I spoke at the Concord for the New York State Food Merchants," Kissinger said in that deep voice. Then he threw in the line, "I hear they fixed the lobby."

"Yes, they did a marvelous job."

We got to the subject of the fee. "Since we're talking one on one," he said, "we don't have to discuss an agent's fee." Right off the bat, I save 25 percent. We set a date.

I had to sell Dr. Kissinger, but one thing I never have to sell is golf at the Concord. The Monster is among the fifty top courses in the country.

A PGA tournament at the Monster
golf course.

I ran into Davey Johnson, manager of the Mets on an all-star break back in 1983. He played the Monster. "How'd you shoot, Davey?"

"Bob," he said, "I'm gonna go out tomorrow and bring that course to its knees!"

Next day, I saw him again. "Davey, how'd you shoot?"

"Ninety-four."

MIKE CASTELUZZI: The Monster is beautiful as well as challenging. Talk about a walk in the park—there are deer close to the fairways and greens, dips and vistas are everywhere. There have been some big name pros, Ed Furgol, Jimmy Demaret, Hubie Smith, whom I replaced. We attract many Japanese golfers because in Japan there are very few courses, and membership in a club is in the vicinity of half a million dollars, and they pay about $300 per round.

ROBERT TOWERS: A while ago a jet was chartered by twenty-four Japanese tycoons. They came into JFK on a Thursday. They were limousined or helicoptered to the Concord. They played thirty-six holes on the Monster. Three days later back to JFK, back to Tokyo. The Orientals have come to the Catskills and fill up the Monster and the International. They are the source of 40 percent of the Concord's golf income.

One weekend there was the third annual reunion of a Korean medical school. I sat with a couple of kids: horn-rimmed glasses, gray slacks—traditional prep school uniform. "Where do you go to school?" I asked one of them, "Choate?"

"Mister, you guessed it."

"What are you doing here?"

"Our fathers, who are doctors, *think* they can play golf."

One day Bill Cosby called me. "Coach," he said, "I have something you can't refuse."

I listened.

"If you will pay my air fare, I'll come down to the Concord and play a mixed doubles."

"Fine," I said.

"Who do you have?" he asked.

"You know Vitas Gerulaitis? His sister, she's a nationally ranked player who's on tour."

Robert Towers (right) poses with his tennis entourage at the Concord. From left to right: Irving Wilensky, father of Concord head pro Gary; former number one U.S. player Ham Richardson; former Wimbledon Champion Chuck McKinley; Gary Wilensky; National Junior Veteran's Champion Tony Vincent (with dog); Butch Seewagon.

"Okay," he says. "Who else do you have?"

"Mary Carillo. She does Wimbledon. She's the most articulate spokesperson of tennis."

"That's great," he says. "Who's the fourth?"

I rubbed it into him because of that "coach" business. I said, "Here's one you can't refuse, a little lady from Harlem who took up the game at fifteen. Great natural athlete. She won Wimbledon, she won the U.S. Open . . . Althea Gibson."

Dead silence.

They play the match. They play an eight-game set. The score is like 5–2 or 4–1 as we change sides on the odd game. I lean over to Althea. "*You* know who you are. But *they're* here to see Cosby win."

"Bob," she said, "he may be the greatest comic in the world on stage, but did he ever win Wimbledon? Did he ever win Forest Hills? Just because they're here to see him win, for that Í'm gonna whip his ass."

Sure enough, she whipped his ass. I couldn't get her to dump.

Bill had flown into Sullivan County International Airport, about ten miles from the Concord. I sent out the limousine, a Cadillac a block long. During the match somebody usurped the limo, and the only car we could get was a lousy Buick about ten years old. It came driving around the back of the tennis courts. Cosby takes a look at the car.

"Coach, how do you like that? You come in like a lion, and you go out like a mouse."

STEVE WHITE: In the early '80s, when Bill Cosby was performing at the Concord, I played with him in a doubles exhibition. I oversee the largest tennis facility in the world, and I've taught plenty of celebrities, but still I was nervous with the big crowd on hand. But Bill was relaxed and kidding around. I guess 1,000 people is an intimate gathering for him.

ROBERT TOWERS: I *said* there'd be a tennis revolution. The four courts weren't enough—they became eight. Then a building of eight indoor courts. Then along came conventions. I said, "Hey, wait a minute. We got the fire chiefs' convention at the Concord. We got fire trucks. We can bring them inside. You know the ceilings on tennis courts. The indoor courts became the site for trade shows: the New York State Food Merchants, the garden people, the seed people, the hard hats—construction people bringing in their heavy gear and such.

IRVING COHEN: During World War II, Arthur Winarick had the first convention up here for the Jewish war veterans. We were at a peak with guests at that time and charging about $30 a day. Mr. Winarick cut the rate and had the convention midweek. Lillian Brown came to him. Murray Posner's father from Brickman's came to him. "What do you need conventions for?"

He said, "Someday the war is going to be over and we'll all need conventions. I'm going to start with this one so I can build on it."

STEVE DELLA: When I began working on the social staff over twenty years ago, the hotel was mainly geared to individual guests. But today conventions are a big part of the business. As entertainment director, I sit down six, eight months before a scheduled convention with the head of the group and plan out what kind of acts they want. For a group like the Knights of Columbus, a Jerry Vale or an Al Martino works well.

Day after day the hotel goes through total transformation. We have 2,000 people from the Knights of Columbus check out on a Sunday afternoon. And then 2,000 people from the Cantors of America or the Elks or a couple of thousand hairdressers check in on a Sunday night.

BILLY VINE: Narcotics Anonymous had a convention here. There were motorcycles parked outside and guys with distinctive tattoos inside. They put down the needles and the spoons, and they came to talk about that whole experience. It was such a draw, we had to keep the coffee shop open twenty-four hours a day. Talk about a switchover: when they came up it was the last day of Passover, and a few of the religious guests had a time intermingling with those people.

ROBERT TOWERS: Ever since I was a kid—my parents came from Minsk—I was brought up with the knowledge of my background, my traditions and all. I can tell you I raised millions in the Catskills over the years for Israel bonds, UJA, Youth Aliyah. I brought Haganah up to Grossinger's for fund raising. The Jewish Theological Seminary said, "You raised money for Israel bonds, but what better way to support the people of the book than by raising money for us?"

I said, "Come on up, and I will raise money for you."

All of those fund-raising events were emotional experiences, but none was as moving and memorable as the Lodz ghetto survivors' reunion.

GORDON WINARICK: The survivors came from all over the country. They wore identifying tags that said things like "I had a sister . . ." People met friends, neighbors, even relatives they thought were dead all these years. You heard their stories, saw them with their children, grandchildren. It was unforgettable.

ROBERT TOWERS: It was a magnificent living memorial. There were speeches, the reading of telegrams from members of Congress, from the president of the United States. And when we brought up survivors for the lighting of candles, people who have lived in America for ten,

twenty years who came up with their children, their sons and daughters-in-law, their grandchildren, you had to laugh and cry at the same time. For three days, we were telling the world we will never forget.

GORDON WINARICK: That reunion is one facet of the whole experience. I've seen so many facets since I was a kid amongst the crowd listening to my Uncle Arthur Winarick expound on his dreams.

GEORGE PARKER: I remember when all the property around here was open space. I remember the old wooden structures, the smaller buildings called the Continental, the Congress, the bungalows here and there, the old baseball field, the shuffleboard court, the four clay tennis courts. What would my grandfather think of it all now?

ROBERT TOWERS: The Concord was the upstart, but it passed every other established hotel. Bigger, bolder, brassier. They used to say Grossinger's was the Ivy League. Well, the Concord became the Pac Ten. USC may not have the tradition of Harvard and Yale, but brother, it's got to be contended with.

SIX

THAT'S THE FLAVOR

JERRY WEISS: When I was a young boy growing up in prewar Germany, we all thought a performer was something special. I've always felt that way. If you can stand in front of a thousand people and they listen to you, you must have something that other people don't have.

HOWARD RAPP: My Uncle Charlie used to say, "You can slap a soprano, you can belt a baritone, but never hit a comic."

JERRY WEISS: There are comics who create and those who rattle off the same thing night after night after night; they range from brilliant to unbelievably stupid.

ALAN TRESSER: I came out of the Lower East Side to the Catskills in 1937, and I'm the last of the old time tummlers in the Mountains, doing my thing at the Fallsview Hotel. They call me The Professor. I think it's because I make them think.

A couple came over to me. "You're a wonderful MC. But that guy who blows the Harpo Marx horn and that loud whistle, the one who wears all those weird outfits and does those lousy impersonations— we don't like him." They thought I was two different people. "Okay," I told them, "I'll straighten him out."

I've been doing Simon Sez longer than anybody in the Mountains. I do an hour with the crowd—there can be as many as 200 to 400 people—and I'll get them going. I start with my whistles. I have three of them. One sound is for kosher, one sound is for nonkosher, and one doesn't blow. That's for people who don't like noise.

For years, I did Simon Sez with birds that I bred and raised. I read about bird training in books and taught myself how to do it. I'd get a bird from a nest, and as far as the bird was concerned, I was its parent. Most of them were blue jays, and I named them all Melvin. I'd say to the bird, "Melvin, what do you do when you see a cat?" and the bird would lay over on its back. At the command "Simon Sez bring me a cigarette" the bird would bring me a cigarette. Once a bird was flying over with my cigarette, and a lady looked up from sunbathing. "My God," she said, "I just saw a bird carrying a cigarette."

"You had too much sun," her husband said. "Go back to sleep."

I've done Simon Sez with everyone—even the FBI guys who were around when President Johnson stayed at the Nevele. They prided themselves on their reflexes, on razor-quick brains. But they were no match for the Professor. I toyed with them, played with them, and got them out, one-two-three. "Stick to your knitting," I told them. "Keep an eye on the president."

Once I did Simon Sez for Arthur Winarick at the Concord. I told the crowd, "My boss is Winarick, and he has a dog called Tonic. Winarick calls him, 'Here, Tonic; here, Tonic.'" The joke is that Winarick, besides owning the Concord, also invented Jeris Hair Tonic.

"I love that," Winarick said.

"Could you pay me?" I asked.

"Love has nothing to do with paying."

Hotel owners are great with one-liners.

Catskill audiences never seem to tire of Simon Sez. Lou Goldstein gets the crowd at Grossinger's going.

I've been at the Fallsview since 1950. My boss, Ben Slutsky, once asked me, "Are you having a good time?"

"Yes," I told him.

"Could you see that the guests join you once in a while?"

My shtik is totally ad-lib. I have no materials, no routine. I do life. Humor is universal.

I hear people say things like, "Thank God it's raining; we don't have to sit in the sun anymore."

A couple talking to each other. The wife: "Another meal? We've got to have another meal?"

The husband: "You don't have to eat."

The wife: "But we're paying for it." I hear those lines, and I put them away. I couldn't think of them even if I wanted to.

Ben Slutsky asked me to write a song for the Fallsview. This is it:

It's your Fallsview, it's your resort.
The baseball and the handball, and the tennis courts.
The rowboats, and the paddles, and the oars—
All of this is yours.
It's your forest, the bushes, too.
The pine trees and the maples all belong to you.
The flora and the fauna and the flowers—
All of this is yours.
Now it's true the Slutskys own the title.
It's true they're raking in the dough.
But little do they know (altogether now—ho, ho, ho)
It's your Fallsview, it's your little lake.
So anything you want, you just go right ahead and take.
Take the napkins, take the tablecloths, take the pillows
from the bed.
It's your Fallsview, don't be bashful, go ahead and take.

MAL Z. LAWRENCE: Like everyone else, I started in the Catskills. Here's an example of my shtik:

"It's so nice to be here at the Raleigh Hotel. This is the end of a career, ladies and gentlemen. Please, on your way home, leave a stone on top of my car."

Two guests talking:

"How about a walk?"

"Where?"

"Well, outside."

"Outside? They have an outside here, too?"

"Yes. We'll walk outside here. We'll go down to the front. We'll look at the parked cars here. Maybe we'll take a walk over to the fence. We'll look at the fence here. Maybe another person will be walking by. Maybe we'll go to the security booth they have here."

I do the lobby, the elevators, and finding your room. Often room numbers don't follow one another, consecutive numbers can be far away from each other. Because they're always adding on wings, room 186 and room 187 can end up being four stories apart. Room numbers are always screwed up, and it's a source of inside humor.

"People check in here. They give you a key, and a map, and a guide. They tell you how to get to the room. You turn away from the desk, and they wave bye-bye.

"People look at each other. 'Which way did they say?' You go left, you go right, go up to the pool, go near the pool, two more upstairs, two more downstairs . . .

The fountain at the entrance to the Concord's Imperial Room. Regulars prided themselves on how many acts they walked out on.

"People walk this way the whole weekend. They read the signs on the wall. Did you ever see the people that get lost here? They look at the signs on the wall: '444–963. They have nine floors in this hotel?'

"The elevators are the greatest in the world here—so unusual. If you want to go to the third floor, you press 6 and walk up half a flight. You don't have to know the floor you're on, the combination is more important. People know, because you see they build a new building over an old building they took out for a new building where the old building used to be, took another building, put it on top of that building . . . This is the Rubik's cube of hotels we're in here."

FREDDIE ROMAN: I started in the Catskills in the late 1950s at the tender age of seventeen as master of ceremonies at what was a very little hotel at that time, Homowack Lodge in Spring Glen. I refer to my origins in my shtik:

"What a thrill to be here at the Concord tonight because I started up here in the Mountains twenty-nine years ago at a little hotel called Homowack Lodge just thirty miles from here, and look how far I've come in this business—thirty farkakte [shitty] miles!"

For Jewish audiences: "You know if you come up here in July and August, there's an anti-Semite who works for the highway department. He lives in Goshen, New York, and every year on June 30, he pulls out 300 or so orange rubber cones. They squeeze the Jews into one lane, and that's how it is for the whole summer. After Labor Day, they take the cones away."

Here's another standard:

"This fellow checks into a hotel with his wife. He goes to breakfast, goes to Simon Sez, eats lunch, lays around in the pool, rows on the lake, plays softball, eats dinner, goes to the early show, then goes to the late show, then goes to the coffee shop.

"Finally at four in the morning, the wife says: 'Let's go to bed.'

" 'Why?' he asks. 'Who's appearing there?' "

That's the flavor.

STEWIE STONE: My routine is about growing up on the streets of Brooklyn, going to Brooklyn College and majoring in stickball, going to Garfield's Cafeteria on Flatbush Avenue. I do humorous reminiscences with the audience about their roots—a stream of consciousness, not joke, joke, joke.

With his homespun humor, Sam Levenson (opposite page) always appealed to Catskill audiences. This 1950s performance was given at Tamarack Lodge.

BOB MELVIN: My real name is Melvin Minkoff. When I began, we all changed names. As an older comic now, I talk about younger comics. "You know," I tell the audience, "I finally figured out why the younger comics always ask me where I'm from. They have no car. They want a lift home."

DICK LORD: My shtik parallels what's happening in my life, in their lives. When my kids were in Little League I would do jokes like this: "I went to the game. A kid got a hit. But where I live, they're so spoiled that the kid doesn't even run to first base. His mother drives him there in a station wagon."

That stuff would not go over now. Today it's hipper. It's observations, relationships. I do the impossible and improbable things I actually see.

For example, consider the alternative to a sign in a jewelry store window: EARS PIERCED, WHILE YOU WAIT.

JACK EAGLE: I was always a funny trumpet player, and I worked with famous bands. Alan King was a drummer, Sid Caesar a saxophone player. It was easier for musicians to become comedians because they were used to listening to comedy and they heard other comedians. You all emulate, you steal a couple of jokes, and things start happening. I still play music on my own, but I love doing comedy.

For a while I had a partner, Frank Man. He was also a trumpet player who had worked the Catskills. Our act was Eagle and Man. Martin and Lewis were very popular then and we did that kind of thing, like an updated Abbott and Costello. Yiddish was spoken at home, so I could incorporate it into the act. On the other hand, Frank's mother was a Jewish Christian Scientist and he didn't know any Yiddish at all. He was the straight man, and I was the comedian.

My act today has a lot of nostalgia. I talk about Brooklyn, where I'm from. I do ringalevio, the old pushcarts on 13th Avenue in Borough Park, Nathan's in Coney Island.

BARRY FRANK: I end the shows at the Raleigh by saying, "Good night, ladies and gentlemen. This is yours truly thanking you for being such a wonderful audience."

One night, a while after my little farewell, a lady came running up to me in the lobby calling, "Yoo-hoo, Mr. Truly! Mr. Truly!"

LOU GOLDSTEIN: I tell the people, "I'm nothing without you. You're nothing without me. Together, we're a damned powerful team. But looking at this group, you need me more than I need you."

Most of them laugh, but some sit there and don't crack a smile. I pick on one. I say, "Look at this man. He's a millionaire. How do I know? Well he drove up here in a Cadillac, and a Jaguar got out."

This joke goes over big sometimes: "Two bumblebees meet. One is wearing a yarmulke, the other isn't. The second asks the first, 'Why are you wearing that skullcap?' The first replies, 'Because I don't want to be taken for a wasp.' "

Sometime in the late '40s, Milton Blackstone sent this guy up to Grossinger's. "I was told to report to you," he said.

"To do what?"

"Help with the entertainment."

"I don't need any help," I told him. "I do it myself."

The guy didn't get excited or uptight. He just hung around the hotel.

In the middle of the summer, Harry Grossinger noticed him and asked one of the staff members, "Who's that guest? He's always in the dining room. He keeps gaining weight. Is he here for the season?"

"Boss, he's with Lou Goldstein's staff."

Harry Grossinger came to see me. "What does that guy on your staff do?"

"He doesn't do anything," I said. "All he does is eat here. I didn't hire him, Harry. Milton Blackstone sent him up."

"Get rid of him."

Singer Jerry Vale has been playing the Catskills for years.

The guy eventually left, but first he did a couple of shows for us. He was sensational, better than any of the big stars we had. A genius raconteur with a thick accent, he had all kinds of new material and insights. His name? Jackie Mason.

HOWARD RAPP: One Saturday Jackie called my uncle. "Get hold of Irving Blickstein at the Homowack. I want to give him a free show—the late show. Tell him to pay the comedian and let him go home to his family. And the only other thing you have to do is get me up to the Mountains because you know I don't drive."

I wound up driving my uncle and Jackie. They were in nonstop conversation talking about everything from politics to prostitution.

That night Jackie Mason got on stage and did not do one piece of material. But he did do everything he and my uncle spoke about in the back seat of the car. And he made it all funny.

SHELLY SHUSTER: In 1954, Jackie Mason was one of four resident comics at the Fieldstone Hotel. He got $25 a week plus room and board, and he was allowed to go out and work at other hotels. But the owners decided he was a sad sack, depressing. "That's Jewish humor," I argued. "What do we have to be happy about?"

"Fire him!" they said.

So I had the pleasure of firing Jackie.

"Why me?" he said. "I'm funnier than the other guys."

"Jackie," I said, "as far as I'm concerned, you can work here forever. But the owners say you have to go."

Fifteen years later, he was doing five shows a night.

VIC ARNELL: My first job as a performer was at the Swan Lake Hotel. I had to share a room with the busboys and waiters, and since I was the last one there I had to sleep on a cot in the closet. Clothes were hanging on top of me.

I couldn't deal with that, so I got a job at Charlow's Irvington Hotel in South Fallsburg. They already had a social director, so they gave me a job as an athletic director. Then after I was there two days, they fired the social director. I asked for the job. They said they were planning to interview somebody else. The somebody else was Jackie Mason.

They told me what he looked like, and I stood on the road waiting

The biting humor of Don Rickles goes over well with Catskill audiences.

Marty Allen (left) and Steve Rossi (right), posing here with Dave Levinson, are still regulars on the Catskill circuit.

for him. When I saw him I said, "I'm Vic Arnell. I'm the athletic director, but I want to be the social director. If you walk in and take that job, I will beat the crap out of you."

And he said, "I'll tell you the truth. The job isn't that important. I don't need it. You can keep it. Good luck and good-bye." He turned around and walked away. And I got the job.

KERMIT BUCKTER: Jackie Mason used to sit in the front of Brown's dining room. One night he was having dinner. His girlfriend arrived late. She didn't realize he was there so she passed him by and walked to the rear of the dining room. Jackie stood up and in a voice that everyone in the place could hear, he yelled out: "Kurve—kim aher!" In Jewish, that means "Whore, come over here!"

ESTHER STRASSBERG: One summer, Jackie stayed in a room in our bungalow colony at Esther Manor and paid me $250 for the whole summer, including food. Our agreement was that he would entertain when he could, since he was working out of our place as home base.

LEBA SEDAKA: I must have been dating Neil around the time Jackie was with us at Esther Manor. To this day, whenever I see him, he'll say, "What did you ever see in the piano player?"

JACK EAGLE: Jackie Mason and I met at a gas station once.
He said to me, "You're very funny."

I said, "You're pretty funny, too."

He said, "See? You don't know how to take a compliment."

He's an enigma. He says the Gentiles love him, the Jews are the only ones embarrassed by him.

Catskill humor is Jewish humor that has been going on in Jewish life since its inception. It's often black. The only way Jews have been able to survive all these years is by thinking, by living by their wits. When you're at the bottom, you live by your wits. We're used to the indignity of failure. We're used to rejection. We do things others can't do. They wouldn't imitate their grandmother—it's not nice.

Lenny Bruce spoke the truth, but he was "too true," if you can say such a thing, for the Mountains—too hip, too outrageous, ahead of his time. He used to work the Mountains mostly as a mimic.

STEVE ROSSI: I see the Catskills as basically vaudeville. It's Jewish-oriented comedy that has become more Gentile-oriented. It remains a great training ground for comedians. If you can be a hit here, you have it. Not that audiences aren't nice people, but they know every act, every joke, every big star.

JEFF KROLICK: A lot of people pride themselves on being able to talk about who they walked out on. I overheard a couple of older ladies. "I walked out on Bob Hope," one of them said. "I walked out on Alan King," the other one said.

BOB MELVIN: All the way through the 1960s, there used to be what we entertainers called the Concord syndrome. Lots of guests stayed up all summer, and they were very tough. They were known as the regulars, the ones with the tables up front in the Imperial Room night club. They'd walk in at just at the end of the opening act. That was their mentality: to see a big star and not like him, to have a good time by not having a good time—that was what they wanted to do. They challenged every star who worked there.

ALAN "BLACKIE" SCHACKNER: If an act bombed, if the audience thought the performance wasn't any good, people would start walking out. There'd be a one-door exit if an act was fair. Then two doors, three doors. If an act really bombed they'd use four doors. Ray Charles stands out in my mind: three doors. Maybe he was too hip.

HOWARD RAPP: Sandra Bernhard was booked at the Concord for a singles weekend. The first thing she said was, "I work in concert. I don't want an opening act."

Now especially at the Concord, you need an opening act. People come in late.

The next thing she said was, "I don't need an introduction. I'm just going out."

She went out. She worked about seven minutes, started insulting the audience, talking about Jewish people and bitches and dykes. She got dirtier and dirtier and more and more hostile. The more she did, the faster the people walked out. It turned out to be the biggest walkout the Concord ever had, an eight-door walkout. At last count, there weren't enough doors for the people to walk out of.

ALAN "BLACKIE" SCHACKNER: I've done thousands of shows in the Catskills, worked before drunks, people who have eaten too much, who are tired, can't keep their eyes open. You learn in front of these people how to perform. They were the seasoned audiences.

LINDA HOPKINS: The Catskills were the foundation of my career. My first appearance there, I opened for Allen and Rossi at the Fallsview Hotel in 1958, after Nipsey Russell had heard me sing in a club in Harlem. Right away, I loved working there because of the audiences. It wasn't like you had to show them what you could do. They were always ready to have fun.

I learned so much about performing up there: how to handle the big stage, how to understand what an audience wanted. I found I could look to an audience to get what I need as a singer. Even after I got the role of the church singer in *Purlie*, I'd still do Sunday night shows up there.

JACK EAGLE: Today there's no longer such a thing as a typical Catskill audience. You can have kosher butchers and the New York State militia in the same audience—that's like meat and dairy. I played the Pulaski Society—that's Polish policemen—at Kutsher's. They were sitting next to Orthodox Jews. You can't say, "This joke's for you, this joke's not for you, listen to this, don't listen to that." It's like working the Gaza Strip. If you want a typical "Catskill" audience, they're all in the condos in Florida.

Broadway star Linda Hopkins claims that the Catskills were the foundation of her career. She began working the Mountains in 1958.

DICK LORD: The Catskills has a reputation that the audiences are made up of a lot of elderly people who only laugh at Jewish jokes. That's not true. The Catskills has the same people who go to Atlantic City, Vegas, conventions. The difference is that when you work other places you finish and they applaud, and you get paid and you go home. In the Catskills they applaud and they pay you, but a guy will come up to you: "Let me tell you what you did wrong."

Or: "Excuse me, Mr. Lord. I enjoyed your show very much. A lot of new material—but same suit."

In 1989, I did my act at the Fallsview, but when I finished, they said, "Oh, no, no. Do more."

I stayed. I did more. Another ten minutes. Another twenty minutes. I stayed overnight and played golf the next morning. In the coffee shop at lunch, an elderly man beckoned with his finger for me to come over to him.

"I was in the audience last night," he gives me a little wink. "I'll tell you the truth," he says. "You were on much too long."

JERRY WEISS: Through the 1960s several hotels showcased new talent in the hope of perpetuating the Catskill comic lineage. The Brickman Hotel had a weekly showcase, and the ringside seats were reserved for agents and TV casting people. All the bookers were there. A lot of great talent was showcased: J. J. Walker, Freddie Prinze, Billy Crystal, Fred Travalena. One night, a while ago, a comedienne came on. She was so outspoken, so nutty, so crazy that I said, "She's a nut, you can't book that girl." That was Bette Midler.

An Imperial Room conga line featuring Telly Savalas.

ALAN "BLACKIE" SCHACKNER: At first, most people wouldn't book Liberace. He was a good showman, classically trained with good style but corny and not a great pianist. "We already got a piano player in the band," they would say. He worked at Grossinger's for $25 or $30—and without candles.

But when his one-man show played the Concord on the Labor Day weekend in 1981, a special piano was trucked in from Manhattan and twenty rooms were set aside for his entourage.

JERRY WEISS: The big difference between the entertainers of fifty or even twenty years ago and the ones working today is the pay scale. I've kept a list of all their fees when they played through all the years. Of course comedians were paid peanuts in those days, but the most important thing was the exposure and the experience. Even in the 1950s, comedians only earned from $100 to $300 a night. In 1956, a new comedian by the name of Shecky Greene received $300 at Grossinger's, which was a lot. Do you know what he gets today?

In 1954, Jan Peerce got $1,700 when he appeared on September 5—the high for that season. But Henny Youngman for $200, Joel Grey for $400, and Alan King for $350 also appeared that year. Jackie Mason got $100 when he was at Grossinger's in 1959. I look at my notes: 1967—Stiller and Meara $500, Rodney Dangerfield $175. In 1973, David Brenner was paid $650 for a show. Billy Crystal in 1976 got $1,000.

Jerry Weiss, longtime talent booker at Grossinger's, had his own confidential rating system for performers. Here he poses with the Brothers Zim.

STEVE ROSSI: Amazingly, some of the biggest stars make more money in one night at a hotel here than they do in a whole week performing in Las Vegas.

JERRY WEISS: I used to have my own confidential ratings for performers: 7 was the highest and 4 was the lowest. I'd keep my records on little index cards that I still have. Robert Merrill got a 6+ in 1945. He was pretty damn good. I've got cards on Eddie Fisher from 1948 to 1982. In 1982, I gave him a 6++. Here's Bojangles on Labor Day, 1945: 6. Why not a 7? I don't remember. On July 22, 1945, Jerry Lewis did Victrola imitations, lip sync. In my opinion he wasn't so good. I gave him a 4. A few years later he returned with a young singer. They were good together, and I gave them a 7. The singer was Dean Martin.

I never told the entertainers the ratings I gave them. It was my code. They would never understand it.

It was my job to book the right act for the right audience. In 1947, for example, I had all in one show on the Fourth of July weekend—Pearl Bailey, Phil Silvers, and Sid Caesar. Would I ever book a Jackie Mason for the Grammy Awards with an audience that's 95 percent black? You gotta be crazy to do that.

MARVIN SCOTT: The late George Gilbert was the coproducer of Broadway shows like *Mr. Wonderful*, and he brought the glitz of Broadway to the Raleigh Hotel, which he owned along with Manny Halbert. People like Chita Rivera and Sammy Davis, Jr. came up, and they'd get the red carpet treatment; he would turn over his

Broadway glitz came to the Raleigh when part owner George Gilbert had "Mr. Wonderful," Sammy Davis, Jr., come up as his guest. Sammy enjoyed kibitzing during hot poker games.

Brown's got on the show business map when Bob Hope appeared there in the mid 1970s. Talent bookers Howard Rapp (left) and Arnold Graham pose with the comedian.

apartment, which ran the entire length of what they called at the time the ranch house, to them.

HOWARD RAPP: Around 1976 or 1977, Brown's wanted to get onto the show business map, so we spent more money than we ever had to bring Bob Hope up. He had never appeared in the Mountains except for the time in 1972 when he was at the Monticello Racetrack.

Everyone was in awe of him. He flew in on a big jet to a local airport, and a police escort with flashing lights brought him to Brown's. It was the most excitement ever.

When Bob Hope walked out on stage the audience gave him a standing ovation. Then they sat down and treated him like any other performer. He had to prove himself, but he won them over.

BOB FELDMAN: By getting Bob Hope to appear at Brown's, Lillian Brown broke the ice as far as other big-name performers were concerned. Lillian was able to get Engelbert Humperdinck, Lawrence Welk, Liberace, Sammy Davis, Jr., Steve Lawrence and Eydie Gorme. She always went overboard on entertainment, and some summers she had better lineups than the Concord.

HOWARD RAPP: Jennie Grossinger was better known than Lillian Brown, but Lillian was more flamboyant, more outgoing. She'd be there when the guests checked in. People loved to be with her.

ROBERT TOWERS: Her forte was to sweep around the dining room. "Darling, how are you? How are the three kids? You look so marvelous. You look so great."

BOB FELDMAN: Some entertainers, no matter how much you pay them, won't work your hotel. But Lillian never had that problem. She was loved. To me, she was the queen of the Catskills.

One of the best-loved Catskill performers was Totie Fields, pictured here with Philly Greenwald (left) and Bob Tish.

HOWARD RAPP: One of the best-loved Catskill performers was Totie Fields. The first time I met her was in the early 1960s. She was

working at the Pines, and I went over and introduced myself as Charlie Rapp's nephew.

"Get outa here!" she screamed. "Who needs nephews? I don't need you rotten kids around."

Almost in tears I turned to walk away.

"Where are you going?" she called out. "Come over here. I love you like I love all the other nephews." And she gave me a great big hug.

Totie had her quirks, but she was something special. As a rule comedy doesn't want comedy; comedy wants singers, dancers. But that wasn't Totie's way. The better they were, the more she wanted them with her, the more she cared about them. She was always there to help other comedians and give them exposure.

FREDDIE ROMAN: In 1969 I appeared at the Concord. Totie Fields was in the audience and came backstage at midnight.

"You were just wonderful," she said. "When is the next time you're working Las Vegas?"

"I never worked Las Vegas," I told her. "I've only worked the Mountains."

"What are you talking about? You've got to work Las Vegas." She picked up the phone in my dressing room, then and there, and called her friend in California who managed Juliet Prowse. "Are you still looking for a comedian to work with Juliet at the Desert Inn?" she asked. "I've got him."

There must have been some protesting on the other end. I guess the manager was telling Totie that he had never heard of me.

But Totie continued. "You'll give him $1,500 and his room and you won't be sorry."

Opening night at the Desert Inn, Totie came in with thirty people. After the show she called Steve and Eydie and had them take me out to Caesar's Palace. Being seen by Totie at the Concord was the break that opened doors for me all over the country.

SANDI MERLE: It was Murray Posner's practice to honor stars whose roots were in the Catskills. Each year, he'd have a ceremony at Brickman's for people like Red Buttons, Milton Berle, George Jessel, or someone like Billy Daniels, who began in the Catskills as a very young man.

SETH THOMAS: During the 1970s, there'd be jam sessions at Brickman's till four in the morning. There was a piano in the lobby, in the barn where we played, in the lounge, on the stage, in the old coffee shop.

Every Wednesday Brickman's had a Big Band Night. We had a twenty-two–piece band conducted by Joe Merman, who also played the piano and wrote a lot of arrangements. Musicians from all the show bands used to come, players from famous bands like Buddy Rich and Maynard Ferguson. They all had charts—arrangements—from the gigs that they had done. Everyone was from the city.

DAVE LEVINSON: I had a neighbor in Ulster Heights named Jerry Hershon who in the spring of 1953 took me to a meeting aimed at getting the NBC Symphony to perform at New Paltz.

"I think we can get a good deal for you in Ellenville," I told them. "I have 100 acres right outside of town. I'll give it to you at cost. I'll house the entertainers at Tamarack. And I think we can raise enough funds among the hotel people to have you settle in Ellenville."

That was how we got the Empire State Music Festival going in 1955. We had a tent that seated 7,500, and conductors like Stokowski, Van Beinum, and Ormandy. We put on full operas. *A Midsummer Night's Dream* had an eight-week run. We did *Madame Butterfly* with Doretta Morrow starring. Critics from all the media and people from all over the world came up.

We hung on for four seasons. All told, among the hotels and the storekeepers we raised about $100,000, but it was not enough. It was a disappointment because the idea was really to take the Borscht Circuit out of the Catskills, to be another Tanglewood, see?

BEN PAISNER: I was band director at Sha Wan Ga Lodge through the 1940s and practically to the very end of the hotel in the 1960s, and every Friday night I would conduct band concerts in an outdoor shell. I would rearrange the classics to make them more popular for our guests. We had some wonderful singers like Gertrude Lawrence and Mimi Benzell, who began her career at Sha Wan Ga and sang for us for several summers.

To tell the truth, though, the guests seemed more interested in the indoor activities. Some people called it Shvanga Lodge. In Yiddish, the word means pregnant, and people did get pregnant there up to a point. We had some huge rooms, and we'd put four or five cots in them, and there'd be eight to ten fellows in each room. Although there was security on every floor and we tried to separate the fellows from the girls, if there was an empty cot, we had a hard time deciphering who was where.

DAVE LEVINSON: We had a teenage camp at Tamarack starting in the late 1950s, and that led to making our nightclub a place for the young music groups on Tuesday nights. Kids came from all over. We had the Rolling Stones, the Blues Project, Led Zeppelin, The Who—all the rock groups. We would do about four shows to standing room only. Half an hour on and half an hour to get the crowd out. Kids would fight to get in and out.

SETH THOMAS: They had the battle of the bands every Tuesday at Brickman's. It was rock 'n' roll. One of the rock bands from a local band like the Pines or the Raleigh or Stevensville would come over. There'd be 500 kids around, no exaggeration.

In the late 1950s, folk and rock groups started performing at Tamarack's teenage camps. These young guests are being entertained by a folk singer.

MARVIN WELKOWITZ: Before Woodstock there were rock concerts all over the Mountains. There were thousands of waiters and bus-boys as potential customers. There were those offtime midweek nights. At $10 or $15 a ticket, the promoters of rock groups cleaned up.

At the Gibber Hotel, a 350-count place in Fallsburg, I saw the Blues Project and, two weeks later, Blood, Sweat and Tears. This was 1968. At the Eldorado Hotel I saw the Drifters and the Vagrants. Other groups there at the time were Vanilla Fudge and the Turtles. Woodstock took place the next summer, less than a half hour away in Bethel, New York.

GORDON WINARICK: It was a phenomenon. People parked their cars and walked twenty miles to get there, but from the hotel's point of

In 1968, a year before Woodstock, Blood, Sweat and Tears appeared at the Gibber Hotel. Pictured are David Clayton Thomas (right) and Steve Katz, formerly of the Blues Project.

view, it didn't really affect us. It's like you have a deli in Washington, D.C. Historic things can be taking place a block away, but you have to concentrate on selling your corned beef and frankfurters.

MARVIN WELKOWITZ: A busload came up to our hotel looking for rooms. On that bus was Sly and the Family Stone. Just that weekend the hotel was completely booked—we couldn't take them in. You couldn't get a room then. You couldn't get gas; the Town of Liberty ran out of gas, and the National Guard was directing traffic.

I went to Woodstock against my parents' wishes. They said, "You'll never get out alive. Who knows what's going on there?" Together with two friends, I left about nine o'clock at night, and we drove in a van through the back roads. We saw a couple of acts. One of them was Janis Joplin. It took us almost three hours to get out of there, and I made it back to the hotel about seven o'clock just in time to change and serve breakfast.

DAVE LEVINSON: We had to stop our rock concerts that year because it got unruly with a half million people in the area coming out for music. We had a line of about 10,000 chanting people on the road and about sixteen cops.

After Woodstock ended, the Four Tops came to see me.

"You don't remember us, Dave," one of them said, "but we were the background music for Billy Eckstine when he sang at your hotel."

MAC ROBBINS: I'm still playing the Catskills, and my first contact with the Mountains was 1939 at the Sunrise Manor in Ellenville. In those days, we'd go out into the woods to get branches and leaves off trees to make scenery for shows.

NORMAN LEIGH: I'm kind of a throwback to those times because at the Nevele I'm the booker, the entertainment director, and the master of ceremonies. Once we had magicians, hypnotists, ventriloquists. There was even an act many years ago called the Stanley Woolf Players, a traveling stock company that did plays.

Television hurt live entertainment. People now want to see the acts that have been on TV. If they're not that famous, the guests are not that interested. The younger crowds want the HBO comics. But they haven't been that successful up here so far. They're too fast, their act is not long enough, and they're not used to playing in front of such a large live audience.

BILLY VINE: When I began working backstage at the Concord in the 1950s, people like my father, Vikki Carr, Vic Damone, and Red Skelton would come up. Red is my all-time favorite. He'd spend an afternoon setting up his camera on a tripod, and then he'd take a picture with his arm around each musician and later send those pictures to them.

In Red's time the performers would have their nosh and do their act. The music came out of onstage monitors to either side of the performer. There was one microphone, one person handling the whole production. Now there are thirty microphones.

Singers like Paul Anka and Bobby Vinton will not sing on the hotel's sound system. They want their own, because they know that people who listen to them on the radio and records are accustomed to a certain sound. And if it doesn't sound that way in the Catskills, people will say, "I heard him. He stunk."

Paul Anka came to the Concord in 1965 with four tractor trailers and changed things all around. We needed a forklift to get the stuff off the trailer and many stagehands to erect the set. We needed riggers to put his lighting up. And as the show unloaded and filled our stage, and we brought in his sound and stacked his speakers and erected his runways, I was no longer a stage manager. I had become the theatrical and technical director.

Today it's a whole new world of highly sophisticated onstage monitoring systems. Once upon a time you might have had a projector that was threaded to show a movie or something like that. Then it evolved to video screens on tripods, and performers gave cues to trigger things. Now videos are preset. The dimming of a light is just one of the ways we set off a video and get it rolling.

Sometimes all this technology can be hazardous. A couple of years ago we had Julio Iglesias. Massive set, ambitious production. He says to the audience, "I'd like to show you the video of me with Willie Nelson. It's 'To All the Girls I've Loved Before.' "

Screens come down electrically, and the video plays. Lights are programmed to change electrically in different hues and different brightnesses. The people watch. It's good. It's over.

He says, "Did you like it?"

They applaud.

"Would you like to see it again?" More applause. "Play the video again," he says.

The man did not know what's going on. How can you play it again? The leader of the video has pulses that cue the screen for the motors to come on. What we are talking about is a long rewind and recue. So his technical director took a backstage announce mike and clicked it on and said, "Mr. Iglesias, there'll be at least a five-minute delay for the tape."

Iglesias says, "So we're gonna wait."

Now five minutes is a long time to wait, especially on a Saturday night in the Imperial Room.

We had 800 pounds of dry ice prepared in machines to create an effect for him to dance on clouds with a girl who'd been flown in on a helicopter and was waiting in the wings ready to go on. But he never came to the wings to get the girl, and the 800 pounds of dry ice melted.

HOWARD RAPP: Who knew from all this technology years ago? Today, it's part of the scene. By the same token, who knew from psychology years ago? Today, we have to take it into account.

A few years ago, we thought we'd booked the perfect act for a kids' Christmas show at the Pines, a trained chimp. Before he went on, the chimp shook hands with the owners backstage. Everyone thought he was the cutest thing.

Then it's seven o'clock, and the act goes on. Kids and their parents are in the audience. The MC introduces the chimp and the trainer. They do a couple of tricks. The kids love it.

All of a sudden, the chimp gets ahead of the trainer, grabs a little kid ringside, picks him up, and slams him down on the ground. The trainer quickly got into it, and fortunately no damage was done. Order was restored.

Later, we found out that the trainer and his wife had separated a few weeks earlier, and the chimp had been shunted back and forth between the two. That night was the first time the trainer had worked with the chimp since his marriage broke up. Little did we know, the star of the show was the product of a broken home who took advantage of his first opportunity to act out.

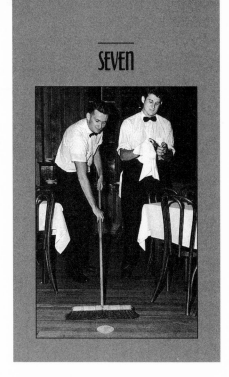

SEVEN

ORDER EVERYTHING

ELAINE MARKSON: The attention to food—it's part of the vision of America as the horn of plenty, part of the pomp and circumstance of making it in the New World. The Catskills were the Jewish version of the country club or first class on the ocean liner. You'd order everything on the menu because you never knew what you'd like. In this way, you got your money's worth.

MAL Z. LAWRENCE: Food is a focal point, where everybody meets. The dining room is almost like a church, only it's not a place to pray but to talk and eat. It's a very friendly thing to do; everybody likes to eat.

In the beginning the Catskill hotels were predicated so much on the food. The guests may not have been crazy about the entertainment, but they knew they could get a square meal. You always heard, "How was the food?"

MARVIN WELKOWITZ: In my time as a waiter it was gimme-gimme-gimme, and the food would keep on coming out. Whatever you wanted, blintzes or fish or bagels, it kept coming. They ordered three or four of everything.

DAVID RICHTER: You order everything on the menu, and every choice comes out on a separate plate. By the end of the meal, you can't see any of the other people at the table because there are eight stories of plates piled up in front of you, with leftovers of the eight main courses you ordered.

PRECEDING PAGES

RIGHT: The vision of America as the horn of plenty was exemplified in Grossinger's buffet. LEFT: In the 1950s, Holy Cross hoopsters were waiters and busboys at Tamarack and did their share of polishing and sweeping.

MAL Z. LAWRENCE: One of my routines is the dining room scene:
"You know it's lunch because they see that other people are beginning to move. In the dining room, people who haven't read a newspaper in years begin to study the menu.
" 'Apple juice, apple juice. Who wants an apple juice? Apple juice, tomato juice, who wants? What kind of juice do you want? Who wants a schav? You want a schav? Wanna schav?
" 'You want a borscht? Potato? No potato? One potato, two potato? Garni? What is garni? Did you ever eat garni? Jellied yellow pike . . . Uhgghhh.'
"The more you read, the less you know what you want. People are really confused now. They look at each other with desperation. They say the same thing at every table.
" 'What are you going to get? You want to share something?'
" 'Come on, we'll split something. I'll have a half of yours. You'll have a half of mine. Because really, I couldn't eat the whole thing.' "
And then there's "For later."
" 'These are for later—these Danishes. No, these are not for now. They are for later. We'll have them with coffee November 23rd.' "

JACKIE HORNER: The Grossinger menu was loaded with an overwhelming list of choices, but everyone understood that it was only

BREAKFAST

MENU

KUTSHER'S COUNTRY CLUB

Menu

FRUIT	CHILLED IMPORTED HONEYDEW MELON SLICE
APPETIZER	CHOPPED CHICKEN LIVER, GARNI
SALAD	COLE SLAW, VINAGRETTE
	TRAY OF ASSORTED TABLE SOURS
SOUPS	FLUFFY MATZOH BALL SOUP
	CONSOMME WITH FLAKES
	CLEAR BROTH

CHOICE OF ENTREE
**ROAST OLD FALLS STUFFED HALF SPRING CHICK...
NATURAL GRAVY
**BRAISED TENDER SLICED BRISKET OF ...
PAN GRAVY
BRAISED CHOPPED SALISBURY P...
ONION SAUCE
SAUTEED CHINESE PEPP...
STEAMED RICE
HUNGARIAN ST...
**BAKED ...
**RO...

What's Happening

GOOD

E
V
E
N
I
N
G

FRIDAY
JULY 14/89

* * *

8:30pm
SEMINAR:
"TAX ADVANTAGE
INVESTMENTS"
/SHEARSON,
HMAN & HUTTO...

EGGS AND OMELETTES

Scrambled
Fried
American Cheese
Plain
Jelly

...-Chip
Poach...
Loz...

Cream Cheese
Onion
...d any Style

HOT

FRUIT

Orange Juice	Melon in Season	Prune Juice
Tomato Juice	Berries in Season	Apple Juice
Pineapple Juice	Grape Juice	Half Grapefruit
Kadota Figs	Sliced Bananas	Baked Apple
Stewed Prunes	Grapefruit Juice	...Orange

APPETIZER

	Pickled Salmon	Pickled H...
Matjes Herring	Smoked Salmon	Chinoo...
Anchovies	Boneless Sardines	Bris...
Nova Scotia Salmon	Herring in Wine Sauce	
Baked or Fried Herring		
Scotch Kippers		

HOT CEREAL

Wheatena

Oatmeal

COLD CEREAL

	Rice Krispies
Corn Flakes	Sugar Pops
Pep	Sugar Frosted...
Puffed Wheat	Shredded W...
Raisin Bran	Cheerios
All Bran	

No Fried or Grilled Orders...
Main Dining Room Will Close Promptly at 10...
Late Continental Breakfast ser...
Kosher Parve Margarine S...
Room Service Charge - 50...

The New Tamarack Lodge

Grosinger's

Breakfast

The Smart Country Club at Greenfield Park

GOOD EVENING

CHILLED MELON IN SEASON   DINNER
NEW DILL PICKLES

* * *

CHEF SALAD WITH CREAMY GARLIC DRESSING

* * *

POTAGE A LA REINE
CONSOMME WITH NOODLES
CLEAR BOUILLON EN TASSE

* * *

ROAST PRIME RIBS OF BEEF, AU JUS
ROAST STUFFED BREAST OF VEAL, PEACH GARNI
OVEN BAKED CRUSTY CHICKEN WITH CRANBERRY COMPOTE
BOILED FILET OF BOSTON BLUE FISH, LEMON WEDGE
BOILED BEEF FLANKEN L'ANGLAISE
STEAMED CHICKEN IN THE POT WITH GARDEN FRESH
VEGETABLES AND MATZOH BALL
ROAST PHILADELPHIA CAPON
...TH GARDEN VEGETABLE DINNER

...LI POTATOES   BROCCOLI SPEARS

* * *

ASSORTED FRENCH PETIT FOUR PLATTER
GOLDEN SPONGE CAKE
CLOVER HONEY CAKE
SUGAR BOW TIES
FRUIT FLAVORED JELLO

* * *

ORANGE PEKOE TEA   ICED TEA
...OD AVAILABLE ON REQUEST..SEE MAITRE D'

...T. 16, 1989   CHUMMY DOLAN, MAITRE D'
BARBARA, HOSTESS

meant to be a rough guide. For breakfast, there were seven varieties of herring alone: baked, pickled, kippered, marinated, fried, tomato, matjes. Someone once asked Sylvia Lyons, the wife of Leonard Lyons, the *New York Post* columnist, how to slenderize at Grossinger's. Sylvia's response: "Go home."

MARVIN WELKOWITZ: Grossinger's used to have tours of the kitchen. I went on it once. It was one of the biggest kitchens of any resort hotel in the world. The figures were staggering: on a summer day, 3,000 rolls, 4,000 pounds of meat and poultry, 15,000 eggs, 250 gallons of soup, 7,500 cups of coffee, 400 quarts of juices, and 2,000 pieces of melon. Their menu was the best I'd ever seen and sampled in the Catskills—the variety, everything. It was top quality.

ERNIE HARING: Food was very simple in the shtetl—a herring, a piece of bread—particularly in the area where the Grossingers came from. That's the region of the Baal Shem Tov, the mystic preacher who founded the Hasidic movement. Religion was the big thing. People lived all week on herring and bread, or whatever, and saved up for Shabbos. And then—ah, *then!*—they had their chicken, their challa, whatever they could manage.

For so many people who came over, America was not the Golden Land, at least not right away. Was it any better than the old country? I don't know. Maybe a little better, but not much. They had to bargain for a piece of fish, fight for it. But they were used to making do, conserving, doing without.

Now, they were able to find a Shangri-la, an ideal, a place that was away, a place that was not a tenement, that reminded them of their old hometown—but with something their hometown did not have. Even more than the food itself, it was the elegance of being served. The elegance of asking for doubles, even if not eating it. Even if just tasting it and saying "nah." That was the luxury of it all.

People who had simple jobs and saved up for weeks just to come to a place like Grossinger's were kings and queens there. They could order whatever they wanted. If it wasn't to their liking, they could send it back without any embarrassment. The customers were 1,000 percent right even if they were wrong. This was their chance to be aggressive, to assert themselves for a change.

The people who came up may not have ever eaten in any elite

restaurants. Here they were served with grandeur. Every night was a banquet. There was the dressing for the occasion, the coming in and looking around to see what others were wearing, what others were doing, being on their best behavior. The activities were actually secondary; it was the food that was paramount.

MARVIN WELKOWITZ: I used to drive in with my father to the Washington Market in New York City, like Paul Grossinger did with his father. We would load the pickup truck with fruits and melons. Then we'd go to the Fulton Fish Market—get our stuff there and come back. We did that every two weeks or so. Later on, we would go to the Hunts Point Market. My father would walk down the line and mark his initials: "JW," "JW," "JW."

"I want this," he'd tell them. "Those honeydews, these cantaloupes, that crate of watermelons."

Then we'd load up and back to the Mountains. We'd leave the hotel before breakfast and make it back just in time for lunch. It was exhausting, but I'd have to put my white shirt on and serve.

MAL Z. LAWRENCE: I remember the announcement "The tearoom is open." There were no coffee shops at first. The hotels themselves supplied cake and cookies. Before you knew it, the tearoom started to serve pickled herring, lox. It became the eagerly awaited fourth meal. Every mother would say, "Eat! Eat! We're paying for it."

LEBA SEDAKA: · In the late 1950s at Esther Manor, we added an indoor swimming pool, a real nightclub, and a coffee shop. The coffee shop caused quite a commotion with the guests because it meant there would no longer be a tearoom. They actually started a petition. The guests used to eat in the tearoom: it was an extra meal and it was free.

MAL Z. LAWRENCE: When people checked out after lunch at Esther Manor, Esther Strassberg would give them a box lunch to take along— so they shouldn't be hungry in the car. That's the Jewish mother.

DAVE LEVINSON: In January 1933, Mom, Pop, and I were in Miami, and we went to see Leo Robinson, who was president of the Mercantile National Bank. He insisted we come out and meet his staff. He told

all his employees how as a boy, he had worked for a baker in Wood-ridge, New York. "And this woman," he said, pointing to Mom, "would never let me out of the yard when I delivered bread to her without giving me breakfast. I remember how angry my mother used to be when I got home because I had no appetite." That was Mom.

ERNIE HARING: In the old country, it was the man's role to keep alive the faith, to study. And the woman had to sustain him and the family. So the mother ran everything, she was the provider, the nourisher, the feeder.

JACK EAGLE: So many women ran the hotels in the Catskills, strong women like Jennie Grossinger, Lillian Brown. It came out of that old-country tradition where the woman ran the business and took care of all the practical matters so the man could study.

DAVE LEVINSON: Mom knew how to make something out of nothing. We hired a new chef years ago. Right away he wanted 40 percent cream, the heavy sweet cream. When regular cream was 10 cents a quart, this was 40 cents. He wanted imported olive oil, only the best.

Mom would say to him, "Sam, it's no trick to take a diamond and make it look like a diamond. The trick is to take glass and make it look like a diamond."

BERNIE COVE: Phil and May Schweid were still running the Pines when I began as maitre d' there in 1961. May watched her business; it seemed she worked twenty-six hours a day. She could talk to dishwashers and chefs, and she could handle anybody in the kitchen. And in those days that wasn't easy for a woman to do. They say May was another Jennie Grossinger. Maybe, but she worked harder.

JERRY WEISS: Malke Grossinger was a real bubbe, a real grandmother. Ach, she was the kind who said, "You're hungry? Come in and eat."

ERNIE HARING: She was about 4'10", emaciated-looking, but there was always a gleam in her eye. She wore a brownish shaytl—a wig of the kind married Orthodox women wear—black boots, and always a benign sweet smile like she was walking with God. And her mission in life there was to get the daily minyan together— the ten men you need for a religious service—and to go around like a little squirrel to see that the dairy and meat dishes were not mixed.

SAM ANDIMAN: In the 1950s, when I tended bar at Tamarack Lodge, I used to see Max "Pop" Levinson go through the kitchen and dining room at mealtime. He would check the settings to make sure the dairy meal had dairy plates, and the evening meal—which usually was meat—had meat plates. If it wasn't done right, he'd shake up the whole table, and the waiter would be moaning as he redid the entire setting.

ERNIE HARING: Lew Jenkins was training at Grossinger's for a fight against Henry Armstrong around 1940. He fooled around a lot and eventually lost the fight. He was very bitter, and when the press asked why he did so poorly, he said it was because he ate kosher food.

Now this really went against the grain of Dan Parker, who was a columnist for the *Daily Mirror*. He wrote a great column,

Malke Grossinger, Jennie's mother, was the kind who said, "You're hungry? Come in and eat." Here she stands in front of her son-in-law Harry.

calling Jenkins a despicable ingrate. This defense of kosher cooking was enlarged and put in the main dining room.

SAL RICHARDS: Before I came to the Jewish Catskills in 1972, I worked the "Boccie Belt"—places like the Villa Maria in Greene County. What did I know from kosher? I went into the dining room and ordered a steak with a glass of milk. The waiter said, "You gotta be kidding."

"What do you mean? Are you out of the stuff?"

I learned quickly: no milk with meat.

IRVING RUDD: As the story goes, Morey Amsterdam was a guy who loved cream in his coffee, but couldn't get it at Grossinger's with the meat meal. So he bought himself a fountain pen and filled it with cream. Whenever they served him his coffee at the end of a meat meal, out came the fountain pen. A couple of little squirts and he was all set.

THERA STEPPICH: The non-Jewish guests love the kosher food. We had the Sons of Italy at the Concord for the first time a while ago. The menu was changed, and matzoh-ball soup was omitted. It almost caused a riot.

JIMMY ABRAHAM: Once Gentiles understand they can get their meat at night, they fall into the groove. Breakfast is a happy diversion from their normal eggs and bacon. They develop a taste for pickled lox, pickled herring, nova, whitefish.

I waited on a Gentile family who came right at the tail end of Passover. The kids had crewcuts and looked right out of Kansas. The matzoh was still on the table, and one of the kids, a little boy about seven years old said, "Mommy can you please pass those crackers?"

IRVING COHEN: A man came up to me one night. "My wife almost choked," he said, grabbing me by the arm. "I'm going to sue the hotel for a million dollars." I went over to his table to see what the problem was.

There is a little metal tag that snaps on to the wing of a chicken to signify that it is kosher. It's called a plummer. When we buy chickens, we pay a little extra for them to remove it, but every once in a great while they miss taking it off. This woman's chicken had a plummer, and there she was holding it up and telling me she almost choked on it.

I thought fast. "What's your name?" I asked. "Your address? Your room number?" She told me.

"Congratulations," I said, "you just won a bottle of champagne!"

"But my wife almost ate the tag," the husband told me.

"The tag was there for a reason, sir," I told him. "Nobody would eat it. People look at what they eat."

I rushed back to my desk and got on the microphone: "Ladies and gentlemen, may I have your attention. I have an important announcement to make. Mr. and Mrs. Sam Weinstein from Cedarhurst, Long Island, have just won a bottle of champagne. Mrs. Weinstein is the lucky lady who wound up with the chicken with the plummer."

Then I went back to the table and asked the couple what kind of champagne they wanted. "Domestic? Imported? Sweet? Dry?"

"Any kind," they become very meek, "but would it be any trouble for you if we could get it in the nightclub?"

BARRY FRANK: They say in Club Med you don't have to bring any money along. Well, you know they got the idea from the Catskills, where you don't need your wallet for anything except shmeering—bribing—to get a better table.

KERMIT BUCKTER: We had a lot of heavy rollers at Brown's. Those were the people who sat at the window tables, the Gold Coast. They got the better rooms and were the better tippers.

Baked on the premises every day: a scene in the kitchen at the Ridge Mountain Hotel.

LOU GOLDSTEIN: The maitre d' says to the captain, "Take this couple to table so-and-so."

If they don't like the table, the guy puts his hand in his pocket and says something like, "I would like a table over there where I think I would be noticed more."

Then he gets, "Follow me, please."

That's why maitre d's and captains always have crooked arms and curled-up hands. But when the money comes out, the arms and hands straighten out pretty fast.

BARRY FRANK: Our hostess at the Raleigh goes by the label "self-taught character analyst." Her specialty is placing you at a table with like-minded guests.

DAVID RICHTER: You come up to the Mountains with one other person, and the maitre d' puts you at a table with ten strangers. You've got to spend the whole time, all the mealtime with ten strangers. And the first thing they ask is, "What do you do for a living?"

I never tell anybody what I do, because no matter who I meet, as soon as they hear I'm a podiatrist, they tell me all about the problems they have with their feet. Once, just when this guy was asking me what I did for a living, my wife ordered a vegetarian cutlet, and he thought she'd said "vetinarian." It turned out everyone at the table had an animal—a cat, a dog, a bird. One even had a horse. You guessed it. They all had problems with their pets.

KERMIT BUCKTER: Working at the desk in the dining room, it sometimes takes me twenty or thirty seconds to look for a table applicable to people who are checking in. I try to regiment them according to age, appearance, etc.

I always wear some kind of jewelry—rings, bracelets. It's part of show biz, I guess. While I'm deciding where to seat the guests, I overhear their conversations. (A lot of people think I'm not Jewish because my name is Kermit, so they speak Yiddish expecting I won't understand.)

Lady says to a man, "Gib im a por tolar." That means, give him a couple of bucks.

The man will answer back, "Er darf nisht keyn gelt. Kik oyf di

tsirung." That means, he doesn't need any money. Look at the jewelry he's wearing.

Sometimes the jewelry has helped me. Same situation. The man answers, "I can't give him five dollars. I'll have to give him ten dollars. Look at the jewelry he's wearing."

Brown's is the place, they say, that made Jerry Lewis famous. As the story was given to me, Mrs. Brown owned the Arthur Hotel in Lakewood. Jerry Lewis was delivering things for a drugstore and made a delivery to Mrs. Brown. That's how they got friendly.

When I first came here, Jerry's father and mother sat at a window table, and he'd come in as crazy as he is today, make believe he was a busboy, and drop a bus box filled with dishes.

BERNIE COVE: In 1948, I was working in a luncheonette in the garment center in New York City and couldn't make a living. A friend of mine suggested we go up to the Catskills for the eight-day Passover holiday to make some extra money. I didn't know from the Catskills— I didn't even know there were hills up here. But I left my wife and baby boy back in Brooklyn, and got a job running the dining room of the LaSalle Hotel in Hurleyville, owned by the Bergers. There were 125 guests.

When I finished the job and came back home, I had $200. Never did I have that much money in my hands at one time. I walked into my little apartment, threw the money on the table, and announced to my wife, "I'm going to get a real job in the Mountains."

For the next six years, we lived opposite the Heiden Hotel in a five-room attic apartment above a chicken coop. We were living out in the country, away from our friends and family. It was a five-hour trip from Brooklyn, and my in-laws would cry every time they visited.

In 1950, I got a job as a busboy at the Concord. That was something special. Irving Cohen had his pick of the litter; you had to be a crackerjack to work there. I stayed on till 1956. And then I moved on to being maitre d' at different hotels. When I heard there was an opening at the Pines, I jumped. It was my big chance.

Having been in this business for so long now, I realize we have a generation that's going out fast. I've known for some time now that I'm hearing things I'm not ever going to hear again—my hand to God. People talk to me about their families, their metabolism rates, stocks and bonds, false teeth, digestive problems. They even complain about

Seating the guests is always a challenge for the maitre d'. This 1952 table at Tamarack attracted a congenial group that included (lower left) Boston Pops conductor Arthur Fiedler.

the noisy people in the room next to them. Jackie Mason got his material from these people. I put a lady at what I thought was a very nice table. She said to me, "You put a person like me at a table like this?"

A guy came over and said, "I got a problem with my relief. My table's too far away."

I moved him down. After the next meal, the guy came back. "Not close enough," he said. I moved him right up to the entrance to the dining room.

After the next meal, he came back again. "Not close enough."

"OK," I said, "I'll put you at a two-seater right outside the men's room."

People come up eighteen years in a row, sit at the same seat, same table. And then one year, they go through a whole personality change.

"I don't like where I'm sitting."

"But you always sat there."

"I'm sitting on top of the wall."

"How can that be?"

"I tell you I'm up against the wall. I don't like it there."

I handle it lighthearted. "OK," I tell the guy, "I don't want you to suffocate."

BARRY FOX: I run into the same problems in the nightclub. Everyone who comes in seems to be blind, or they can't hear, or their tuchis hurt. They all have to sit dead center on the railing.

We used to get this guy at the Nevele; when he came, you knew the season had started. His name was Dewey Feinberg, he always showed up with a group of friends, and year after year he'd book the same table. Other people might say, "Barry, I'd like that table."

And I'd say, "When Feinberg leaves us, you'll get his table."

"What do you mean 'leaves us'?"

"Leaves us for yener velt [the other world]."

But you can't count on people like Dewey anymore.

BERNIE COVE: Never in my wildest dreams did I ever think I'd appear in a movie. But about four years ago I had a part in *Sweet Lorraine*. I come into the kitchen dressed in red slacks and ask, "Who made the coleslaw?" That movie was, as Yogi Berra said, "déjà vu all over again." It was filmed at the old Heiden Hotel that I saw out of my front window. The terms used in the movie like "livestock" for the pickles and salads, the summer romances that weren't meant to be, the tumult of opening the season, the sadness of closing down after Labor Day, the quirks of the guests, the problems these small hotels had in making it from one season to the next, and how most eventually closed down—all of this is true. I saw it. I lived it.

MARVIN WELKOWITZ: There were three or four hotel-employment agencies in Monticello alone. Harold's, in back of the bowling alley, was the main place. It was packed with guys dressed in white shirts and black pants and ties. Harold would say, "Give me six for the Esther Manor. Give me four for the Paramount. The Ridge needs three." It was a madhouse.

There were hundreds of hotels, and kids from all over the city and suburbs went there to get a summer job. They knew they'd take home between $1,000 and $2,000 in salary and tips, enough to pay for college. They put themselves through medical school and law school with that money.

LEBA SEDAKA: My mother would hire college students, preferably pre-med or -law students. They had to be personable and dance with the guests. We had dancing seven nights a week, and a lot of women came up for the season, while their husbands only came up on weekends.

DAVE LEVINSON: When we had college students working as waiters and busboys, Pop would go into their cabin every morning and yell, "Doctors! Advokatn [lawyers]! Shtey shon aroyf [get up already]!"

IRVING COHEN: Some years ago my wife was ill, and our local doctor said to me, "There's one doctor that's the best lung man in the city: Dr. Tierstein, out of Mt. Sinai Hospital. I would suggest you go in to see him."

I said, "Maybe you can call up and get an appointment for me."

He tried, but he told me he couldn't get an appointment. So I figured I'll call and tell the girl I'm coming in. "I'll wait," I said, "but I would like Dr. Tierstein to take care of my wife."

She told me she was sorry, but there was nothing available. So I said, "Take my address and phone number. If an opening comes up, call me. It's an emergency."

She said, "Mr. Cohen, unfortunately all of Dr. Tierstein's appointments are emergencies. He's the professor of pulmonary diseases up here."

Anyway, somehow or other, my name must have been on the desk. Because he came in, saw Irving Cohen, Concord Hotel, and the telephone number. And he said to the girl, "What does he want?"

She said, "He wants an appointment."

He called me personally to arrange to see my wife. I didn't remember him, but he told me he used to work here while he went to medical school.

DAVE LEVINSON: Herman Wouk was a waiter in the children's dining room at Tamarack. He based the setting of *Marjorie Morningstar* on our place, although he changed it into an adult camp.

ART D'LUGOFF: Back in the 1950s, I would hitchhike up on weekends from New York City. My specialty was being a busboy, and my hope was getting a good station.

A world-famous ice skater had come up to the hotel I was working at, and everyone was making a big fuss over her. One day I was running back and forth, carrying things in and out. Suddenly, crash! Boom! Dishes started to fall all over the place. I just happened to be within arm's reach of the maitre d', who grabbed me by the sleeve.

"What happened here?" he yelled. "We spend thousands of dollars to bring a woman like that up here, and look what's going on! Look at all this dreck [garbage], all this shmutz [dirt], this commotion, this awful mess! What do you have to say for yourself?"

I didn't think fast. I only told the truth. Looking him straight in the face, I said, "It's not my station."

Another time I was working at the Laurels Country Club. I struggled out of the kitchen with a big tray filled with hot coffee, iced tea, cookies, cake, strudel, baked apples, halvah, fruit cups, stewed prunes. I was straining to manage the load.

Out in the dining room, someone—accidentally I think—gave me a little nudge. Plop! Everything on the tray landed on the neck and back of one of the guests. I ran into the kitchen with the empty tray. The guy ran after me. I ducked into a broom closet and stayed there for about an hour. I spent the rest of that weekend with one hand in front of my face. I didn't want to get killed.

All set: the dining room at the Ridge Mountain Hotel.

MIKE HALL: While I was a waiter at the Concord during World War II, I used to complain to the manager how lousy the entertainment was. "I could put on a better show with the hotel staff," I bragged.

"OK," said the manager, "do it."

I don't think my boast was serious, but once challenged I couldn't back down. So for six weeks, I worked on a show. I became obsessed with it. I did the book, the music, the lyrics, produced, directed, and was a member of the cast. All the while, I was still a waiter.

My mind was on the show and not on waiting tables, and as a result, the people at my station suffered untold agonies. Rarely did the author/waiter bring them what they had ordered. One lady was particularly distressed.

"Apricots, apricots," she said. "I order chicken livers, steak, herring. It makes no different what. Always he is bringing me apricots." For some reason, in the throes of my authorship, I kept associating her with apricots.

The show, *At Your Service, Please*, finally went on and was the smash of the summer season. It opened in a courtroom where a waitress was on trial for murdering a guest who had the habit of coming in late for dinner. That scene ended with a song called "The Man Who Came to Dinner—Late." The hit number was "I Don't Want to Walk Without You"—a ditty that included twenty-two waitresses and busboys mingling their voices in song and performing intricate dance routines.

After the show, I got called in by the hotel publicity man. The end result? Mike Hall–waiter became Michael J. Hall–Broadway press agent.

MARVIN SCOTT: Bellhops would always deliver meals to the room for people who couldn't get to the dining room. Once over Passover, a friend and I decided we didn't want to eat the food they had for the staff. It was OK but not as good as the food the guests got, so we decided to make our own seder. We went into the kitchen and told them that we were making up a tray for room service and began putting everything together with all the trimmings. We were just finishing up the tray when we heard, "What are you doing?"

We almost died. The voice belonged to Manny Halbert, who we nicknamed Pussyfoot because he'd sneak around and you'd never know he was there.

"Just making up a room service tray, Mr. Halbert," we said.

"That's not the way you put a tray together. This is a holiday. You can't send up a tray like that."

My friend Danny and I looked at each other as Manny started fussing. He picked up linen napkins and put them on the trays. Then he brought out two bottles of wine.

"*This* is what you send up!" he said. We just stood back and watched him.

We picked up the tray and walked out all the way to the back of the property and sat down at a Ping-Pong table and had ourselves a feast.

ERNIE HARING: My best friend was a nephew of Eddie Cantor. We worked together as busboys in Grossinger's, and the head of the busboys was a member of the Grossinger family named Sam Vogel. Sam was a nice guy, sort of a benevolent despot. He would kid around with us, but he made us work.

One day, when the guests had left, he was after us to sweep. "Boyiss, please, sweep up the floor," he cried. But we were fooling

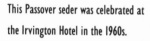

This Passover seder was celebrated at the Irvington Hotel in the 1960s.

around and didn't get to it. "I'm gonna kill you," he said, flavoring his threat with some choice obscene terms. Then he saw Eddie Cantor talking to me, and he yells out, "Eddie Canfer, you are the world's worst!"

Eddie Cantor made no reply, but rose to the challenge. He picked up a broom and began to sweep.

KERMIT BUCKTER: There was a time here when everybody who worked in the dining room was named Moishe, Irving, Sam, Harry. Today I employ upwards of eighty people. Seventy-nine are called Rodriguez. I have to use initials to make a payroll.

MARVIN WELKOWITZ: There are hardly any part-time workers in the Mountains today. You don't get your college students working for tuition anymore. You couldn't make enough money in a summer to cover a year's tuition the way college costs have gone up.

IRVING COHEN: When you had to work to make money to go to school, Sullivan County was a very good place. Today, it's different. The kids don't have to work so hard anymore. I think we're too good to our children.

MARVIN WELKOWITZ: So many summer hotels have gone out of business, but not necessarily because they didn't have the guests. The problem was the help—they couldn't get the summer help. My parents sold the Ridge Mountain in the 1970s and they were three quarters booked for the entire summer. They couldn't get waiters or busboys or dishwashers. They weren't like Brown's or the Nevele with full-time help. They wanted part-time people, and those kind of workers weren't around anymore. Harold's was gone. There was no one left to draw employment from.

IRVING COHEN: We all have trouble getting help. The Mountains are changing. I predict hotel chains will come up here. It's got to go into the European plan, a choice of restaurants: kosher, not kosher. Conventions we'll serve two meals a day. That's the future. A different way of eating. Today people come here not so much to eat, but to enjoy the activities. They eat and they want to get out. They're eating less.

Today the challenge is to produce
gourmet recipes within kosher
restrictions. James V. Farina, former
head chef at the Concord, is seen
here preparing a chicken specialty.

SHARON PARKER: You can say some things have come full circle, but with a twist. In the past guests were given jars of pickled herring to take home. Today they still take home packages of food, but now it's gourmet brownies, linzer tarts, and chocolate croissants from our patisserie.

JAMES V. FARINA: For me the real challenge is to produce gourmet recipes with all the kosher restrictions. I've made artificial sour cream for stroganoff, breast of chicken Wellington, chicken Kiev with margarine instead of butter . . .

JULIE SLUTSKY: Nowadays at the Nevele we serve seafood and non-kosher meat; we don't separate meat and dairy. But we still serve the Jewish ethnic items: matzoh-ball soup, potato pancakes, stuffed cabbage, and, of course, borscht.

MAL Z. LAWRENCE: It may have been the Borscht Circuit back then when little family-style hotels would put a pitcher of borscht on the table, but it's no "Borscht Circuit" anymore. They could have just as easily put out schav. The Catskills could have been the Schav Circuit.

People think borscht is a Jewish dish, but it's actually Russian, made out of beets and served with potatoes. It's so versatile. You can have it hot with meat. You can have it cold with sour cream. It became so popular in the Mountains because so many people who came up there were of Russian descent. Everybody loved it, so they just kept pitchers of it out.

Schav is something else. That's made of sorrel. It's never served in a pitcher; you have to order it separately. I hate it.

BARRY FRANK: I love the Borscht Circuit, and I don't mind the name. I know some people want to hide from it and call it something else—Catskill Land, whatever. But the term "Borscht Circuit" is okay with me.

PAUL GROSSINGER: Seven days a week, fifty-two weeks a year, borscht in a glass was served at Grossinger's. Abel Green, the editor of *Variety*, got on us and coined the phrase the Borscht Belt. Way down deep, we all thought it was an ethnic slur. Maybe it was. But then there were some who took it as a red badge of courage.

The Olympic Hotel, around 1960. Like many other Catskill resorts, it remains only a memory.

EPILOGUE

It is nearly 100 years since the original Russian Jewish immigrants moved up to the Mountains looking for something better than life in the tenements and sweatshops of New York City. Their little farms and modest boardinghouses are long gone. Gone, too, are hundreds of the hotels and bungalow colonies they grew into as the century moved along. Here and there a Moorish structure emerges along Old Route 17, a gabled Tudor peeks out from behind trees down a quiet rural lane, an Art Deco facade of glass and stone crowns a sloping meadow that once was a lawn. Strangely out of place in the surrounding countryside, they are abandoned to overgrown nature or converted to some other use. Grossinger's is a vacant pink castle on a hill, waiting to be reborn. And the once pristine little Sullivan County towns have lost their country charm.

Yet the region still flourishes with a dozen or so ultramodern resorts and their all-inclusive vacation packages. They are the Catskills of the 1990s, they and the health farms, and the retreats, and the condos, and the year-round, all-weather vacation homes now reached via the Quickway in under two hours from New York City; and the clientele is Gentile as often as Jewish.

Only in glistening memory do things remain unchanged.

MARVIN WELKOWITZ: At one point we thought Jay Tanzman would take over his father's hotel; and I would take over the Ridge Mountain—my father's hotel; and Maxie Schmidt's kid would take over the Grand—his parents' hotel; and Zane Morgenstein would take over the Brighton—his father's hotel. We would talk about it lots of times. But I realized it was not to be when I had to wash dishes for 200 people at the hotel because there was no one there to run the dishwasher. And my father was ready to collapse from standing up from five in the morning from cooking the food because he couldn't get a chef that he was willing to pay thousands of dollars for the summer.

NEIL SEDAKA: Esther Manor was sold in 1969 when my mother-in-law took ill and was advised to give up the business. After a time we went back to see it. We walked through the building, and I saw the place where I was married and where I played the piano so many times. I could just make out where some of the rooms had been on the lower floors.

ESTHER STRASSBERG: We went back to Esther Manor in hopes of trying to start the hotel up again. We returned with such high hopes, but what we saw was shocking. The grass was filled with weeds, paint was peeling, the swimming pool was filthy. Oh, the baby that I had taken such good care of was devastated!

MARVIN WELKOWITZ: It was the convention business that really hurt the small hotels and businesses in the Town of Liberty and so many other places. Convention people come up for two days or three days on business. They don't leave hotels for shopping, sightseeing, haircuts.

None of the small hotels really had conventions. They had a resident, not a transient population. Only once a year at our hotel, my father's lodge, the Harlem Benevolent Association—seventy people— came up. That was the convention.

MAL Z. LAWRENCE: Once, up here every tenth of a mile you had your hotel, your bungalow colony, somewhere to do your stolen routines. There were so many good times, simple times. And people laughed easier because they weren't as sophisticated. You didn't have to use so much flash to entertain them. They enjoyed a good comic, a good singer. They seemed more appreciative. Because not everybody had a TV set in those days—they didn't even broadcast all day back then—people seemed to love live entertainment more. Today, they're jaded. They've seen everybody.

With the comics and other entertainers, it's not a fraternity anymore. The Red Apple Rest isn't the meeting place anymore. We had certain hotels like the Raleigh that we used to just fall into, where we would try out stuff late at night, ad lib. We could do that because we were all up here. Now everyone is away. They drive in for the night and fly out.

SOL ZIM: I miss Grossinger's, I miss the kochalayns, I miss the warmth, the real Catskills, being on the road, doing maybe sixty shows a summer, taking my boys along with me, staying at different hotels every night, the old neshomadik [soulful] audiences. The Catskills were a Jewish haven where you didn't have to worry whether the food was kosher, where there was a joyful Jewish experience.

DAVE LEVINSON: Of course I always said Tamarack was not for sale, but I never thought I'd get a customer. But once I got a customer, I sold and I'm very happy about it. I wish the new people lots of good luck.

I live on the property. We didn't sell properties that my house, my tree farm, and several other houses belonging to my family are on. I'm not even a consultant. But we're happy staying put. We don't like to move around too much.

FRED GASTHALTER: The Paramount, my hotel, is the only one that remains in Parksville. The strongest stay, the rest disappear.

ROBERT PARKER: You couldn't give horsewhips and spats away today. You can have the most successful business in the world, but if it's not what people want, you can't give it away. The hotels that have stayed and thrived are the ones that changed with the times. Those that didn't went under. It was just a shaking out. But if you take the total amount of rooms in the Mountains today, I daresay it's probably not a hell of a lot less than thirty, forty years ago. There were a lot of places with fifty, sixty rooms back then.

JERRY EHRLICH: Our two sons run the Pines with us. They came up through the ranks as kitchen workers, bellhops, behind the desk. Someone from the family is around all the time, on the premises, visible to the guests.

    We put everything back into the business. There may not be much money in the bank, but there's expansion, modernizing, changing with the times.

HARRIET EHRLICH: What we learned from my parents is that in this business, you can't stand still. Those hotels that did are out of business. We've had to attract new groups. In different eras, there are different audiences. Today in the winter, we have a young crowd; in the summer, we draw seniors with midweek specials; in the spring and fall, we have ethnic and fraternal festivals, jazz festivals, bluegrass festivals.

JULIE SLUTSKY: The Nevele went from my father, to my brother Ben and me, to our children. I think the Nevele continues to survive and thrive because of our very beautiful setting, but also because we keep putting everything back into the business.

Past and present: the sign to the Nevele and Fallsview in front of the one-room schoolhouse that Julie and Ben Slutsky attended.

TONY MARTIN: I'm past seventy-five now; I've played in all the hotels, and I still go up to the Catskills to work. So I can see how they've changed. You get different people up there now. It was once mostly Jewish, but now there's a mixture of all kinds, from all over. The Catskills is for everybody now.

ROBERT TOWERS: Today there are times I'll look around and "mer ziet nisht keyn yidishe ponim"—a Jewish face is nowhere to be seen. But then, on Passover, Jewish families come from Denver, from Peoria, from St. Louis—from all over the country, all over the world. Sometimes three, even four generations. They want that "tam"—taste—of Yiddishkeit, that sentimentality, that feeling.

IRVING COHEN: The Firemans, twenty people, come up from Wisconsin on Passover. Mr. Fireman says, "I don't think my children know of a shul where they live because there is none." Here for Passover week, he takes his grandchildren to shul, teaches them Hebrew.

DAVID FISHER: When I perform as the cantor at Kutcher's for Passover and the High Holy Days, the hotel is transformed into a synagogue. It's a shul-going crowd. The people come to daven. All the time there is the sound of prayer. For me, the sound behind my back is like great applause at a concert.

I am an Israeli and the child of survivors. On the last day of Passover, we have yizkor [memorial] services, and sometimes people ask me to include the name of a ghetto that I had not heard of before when we do the "El Moleh Rachamim" [memorial prayer] for the souls of the six million Jews who perished in the Holocaust. The time when I am moved the most is when I do the prayer for the soldiers who were killed in all the wars in Israel, because so many of my friends and relatives were killed.

SHIMON FARKAS: I was born in Hungary, the child of survivors. I moved to Israel with my family when I was an infant. My father died there at a young age because he was so sick from being in the concentration camps. I was a practicing cantor for fifteen years in Central Synagogue in Sydney, Australia. Now I come to the Concord every

Rosh Hashanah and Passover. The crowd has a lot of survivors. I still look at the tattoo on my mother's arm, and I identify with them. My mother discovered a cousin at the Concord she hadn't seen in forty years. They lost track of each other after the war and met by accident.

What is it like to daven at a hotel? People make a sanctuary; the dining room becomes a sanctuary during the seder.

ERROL DANTE: The Catskill audience is still often a heritage audience. Even when the younger people come up here, they want to hear what their mothers and fathers heard.

BOB LIPMAN: Many first-timers come up now. But there are still all of those whose parents and grandparents vacationed in the Catskills, and there are roots.

You know what to expect. You call in advance. You know what room you're getting: the same room as the year before. You're welcomed when you come up. You get the same table, the same waiter. The owner comes over to you. She knows your aunt had died or your business had expanded. She knows what to talk to you about.

HELEN KUTSHER: Some guests out of habit go to their rooms first and then let the front desk know they've arrived. If there's a room someone likes, you make sure they get it year after year. If you moved Mrs. Litsky from 635 to 604, she'd go into trauma. Some families don't even return their keys. To me this is not a business. It's something I've grown up with, a way of life.

STEWIE STONE: One of the unique things about the Catskills is the attitude of the hotel owners. I hate to get political, but during the terrible McCarthy era, guys who couldn't get work anywhere else were working up there. Zero Mostel was blacklisted all over the place, but he put bread on his table by working the Mountains. If you're sick or broke, the owners will give you money, and you'll pay them back by doing shows.

MAL Z. LAWRENCE: If you work Atlantic City, you don't mingle with Donald Trump. But the Kutshers, for example, are like family to me. I've made so much money from them, drank so much of their whiskey.

FREDDIE ROMAN: I walk into Kutsher's, I don't go to the front desk. I walk right into the office, sit down on the couch, and shmooze with Milton for an hour or so. Then we go have dinner in the dining room. And that's the same with every one of the owners pretty much. It's not corporate.

FRED GASTHALTER: Sometimes we overbook, like the airlines. My manager, Bella Sarquhar, the only Italian manager of a Jewish hotel, once tried to placate a couple of oldtime regular guests who were shut out of their rooms. She offered to put them up at Howard Johnson's for the night until we could get things sorted out. No dice. She tried to explain the situation to them. She tried to reason with them. They wouldn't listen. Finally she gave up and brought them in to me.

"Freddie," they said, "how could you do this to us? We've been coming up to the hotel for such a long time. We're so upset."

"Upset?" I told them. "You're upset? You should be happy for me that I'm so busy, that I'm filled up."

That got them.

"Freddie darling, you're right. It's wonderful. If only your mother could see you now."

They did me a mitzvah [good deed] and went to Howard Johnson's.

There's a lot of poignancy connected with this business. In the summer of 1989, a little old lady came up to the Paramount with her daughter and a driver. She had been a guest at our place from 1913 to 1917 and then for one reason or another never returned. Her father, a rabbi, had taught Hebrew to my father and his two brothers. She remembered my grandfather.

"I had to come back," she said. "I promised myself that before I died I would come back and see this place I stayed at more than seventy years ago."

SIMON TIMLICHMAN: I was born in a very small town high up in the Carpathian Mountains and came to the United States in 1972. Around a year later, I was up in the Catskills performing as part of a musical group. We went all around the area, doing little shows of Russian folk and Gypsy music in hotels and bungalow colonies. I played the bayan, the Russian accordion with buttons on both sides, and sang. We also had a Russian balalaika player, and a girl and guy who danced.

This gabled Tudor was once the Heiden Hotel.

It was such a surprise to me to see the Mountains. With the propaganda in Russia in those years, I thought I was coming to a stone city; I didn't even think America had mountains or parks or trees. When I came and saw there was everything here, beautiful mountains, I was surprised.

I was impressed with New York being such a Jewish city with Hebrew letters written on stores. Then when I see the Catskill resorts with kosher food, it's impressive, it's like coming from another planet. I met people all over the Mountains who tell me, "My parents are from Russia, I'm from Russia." It seems about 75 percent of the Jews are from Russia. And the rest are from Poland.

I must say this: every time I come back to the Catskills, I feel like I'm coming home.

MAL Z. LAWRENCE: The Catskills are so tightly wound up with my life. I've spent so much time up here that I almost look at it as my own country. I live up here—this is my Hollywood, my Beverly Hills.

ROBERT PARKER: The best years in the Mountains lie ahead. Of course, if you're looking for the glory years of the '30s, the '40s, the '50s, no—it will be different. But the good hotels will continue to thrive. And beyond that, the area will come into its own as an ecological gem. Orange County is going to be a suburb of New York City in just a matter of time. Stewart Airport is going to be the fourth jetport, which will make us accessible to the world. We're at the hub of the northeast, and yet we're still virtually virgin territory. Sullivan County is gorgeous, lush and green. You can drive ten or fifteen miles from the Concord and see eagles. We have deer, bear, we're a leading agricultural region. We have clean air and clean water. Where else can you live with all of this and be just an hour and a half from the greatest city in the world?

GERALD VINCENT: I was born in Kansas City and now live in Los Angeles, but of course I heard of the Catskills before I came up here to dance with the Suzanne Somers show. Who hasn't?

You can tell from the minute you get here that there's so much history. I took the time to sit on the porch at Brown's, looked around, talked to the people. It's like a sanctuary.

MARVIN WELKOWITZ: You know this area goes back a long way. This is Rip Van Winkle country—remember the guy who bowled with the dwarfs and slept for twenty years, and when he woke up everything was different? Well, lots of things have changed. What was the Neversink Inn is now a spa called the New Age Health Farm. Klein's Hillside is an orthodox Jewish camp. Some of the smaller places are camps for Lubavitch and Satmar—Hasidic sects. What was the Belvedere Hotel in Woodbourne is the Sivananda Ashram Yoga Ranch Colony. The Brickman and Gilbert's were taken over by the Syda Foundation. People come there from all over to study yoga, meditate, follow the teachings of their guru.

SETH THOMAS: There are all these ashrams up there, guru ranches; the Hasidim are up there, and they're very spiritual. I've met a lot of psychics up there, mystics, unusual people.

And I've seen things. In 1977, my friend Kevin and I were working at the Brickman when we saw something in the fields. It was about three in the morning, and we went screaming to his mother's bungalow colony because we were terrified.

At first they look like airplanes and blinking lights, and then they move in one direction, and you think they're flying away like an airplane. Then they stop and hover, and move back in the other direction. They come forward and go back. I've seen about three myself although I've never approached them. And I'm not the only one who's seen these things.

I've been coming up here since I was a little kid, and I tell you, there's a lot of spiritual energy in the Catskills. It's a very special place.

ACKNOWLEDGMENTS

A work of this sort could never have been possible without the support, guidance, coaching, memories, and perceptions of so many.

Howard Rapp and Arnold Graham of Charles Rapp Enterprises gave us access to most of the celebrity voices. Insights into the Mountains, political sensitivities, great stories—Howard and Arnold were there for those, too. In the rough and tumble that is show business, these two men stand apart for their gentlemanly qualities and kindnesses.

Robert Towers, the lion of Manhattan, the man who speaks in finished prose, was at once an inspiration and a great coach. His eloquence and insights added immeasurably to this project.

Mike Hall, a whirling dervish of a man, took time out from his busy schedule to direct us onto the right paths.

Our children—Jennifer, Freddy, and Ian—listened to an evolving manuscript, although not always willingly. Now they can read what they heard.

Others whose voices were silent in the book but whose words and assistance helped a great deal include:

Vicki Austin, Dr. Karl E. Bernstein, Polly Bernstein, Sam Bernstein, Dorothy Bokor, Harriet Brahms, Lillian Brown, Joe Childs, Mort Curtis, Ellen Cutler, Joyce Feigenbaum, Ruddy-Ann Friedman, Diane Gardner, Ed Gray, John Hart, Dan Janeck, Chuck Jones, Margo Jones, Howard Kaiser, Caroline Katz, Donna Kelly, Miriam Kittrell, Holly Lipton, Phil Mauro, Marilyn McGinley, Dr. Robert E. Pillar, Cheryl Rapp, Roger Riddle, Shelly Rothman, August St. Anthony, Fiorenza Sigler, Milena Siuzdak, Deborah Sugar, and the staff and guests at Brown's, the Concord, Kutsher's, the Nevele, the Paramount, the Pines, and the Raleigh.

The people at HBJ—Lydia D'moch (designer), Trina Stahl (cover designer), Warren Wallerstein (director of production), and Vaughn Andrews (art director)—added their unique vision to this story. Our thanks to them.

And special thanks to John Radziewicz, our editor extraordinaire. He had unflagging enthusiasm for the project, was a comforting and creative constant, and provided the perfect finishing touch.

SELECT BIBLIOGRAPHY

Joey Adams and Henry Tobias, *The Borscht Belt* (New York: Bobbs-Merrill, 1966)

Tania Grossinger, *Growing Up at Grossinger's* (New York: David McKay, 1975)

Irving Howe, *World of Our Fathers* (New York: Harcourt Brace Jovanovich, 1976)

Irving Howe and Kenneth Libo, eds., *How We Lived: A Documentary History of Immigrant Jews in America 1880–1930* (New York: Richard Marek, 1979)

Stefan Kanfer, *A Summer World: The Attempt to Build a Jewish Eden in the Catskills, from the Days of the Ghetto to the Rise and Decline of the Borscht Belt* (New York: Farrar Straus Giroux, 1989)

Leo Rosten, *The Joys of Yiddish* (New York: McGraw-Hill, 1968)

Michael Strauss, *The New York Times Guide to Ski Areas U.S.A.* (New York: Quadrangle Books, 1972)

Manville B. Wakefield, *To the Mountains by Rail* (Grahamsville, N.Y.: Wakefair Press, 1970)

PICTURE CREDITS

INDEX

Note: Page numbers in *italics* refer to captions. Page numbers in SMALL CAPITALS refer to speakers in this oral history.

Finkel, Feibish, 72–73
First, Harry, VI, 41
First, Lee, xv, 41
Fisher, David, xv, 229
Fisher, Eddie, xv, 31, *36*, 49–50, *50*, 51–54, *53*, 59, 60, 61, 191
Fishman family, 125
Flagler Hotel, 1, 11, 18–19
Flynn, Errol, 40
Food, 202–11, *204, 208, 209, 211, 218*, 219–23, *222*
Forbes, Frances, 19
Forman, Joey, 52
Foster, Phil, 45, 78
Four Tops, 199
Fox, Barry, xv, 130, 215
Francis, Connie, 107
Frank, Barry, xv, 183, 211, 212, 223
Frankel, Morty, xv, 16–17
Friedman, Naomi Parker, xvi, 165–66
Friedman, Rosie, 57
Fullmer, Gene, 59
Furgol, Ed, 171

G

Gale, Moe, 36
Garfield, John, 50, 51, 64, 139, 144
Garland, Judy, 153, 162
Gasthalter, Fred, xvi, 6–7, 121, 227, 231
Gasthalter, Sam, 6
Gasthalter family, 120
Gavilan, Kid, 44
Gaynor, Mitzi, 135
Gerulaitis, Vitas, 171
Gibber Hotel, 198, *198*
Gibson, Althea, 172–73
Gibson, Bob, 166
Gilbert, George, 192–93, *192*
Gilbert's Hotel, 233
Gleason, Jackie, 77
Glenmere Hotel, 79–81, *79*
Gluck's Hillside, 150
Goldberg, Max, xvi, 18
Goldstein, Carl, 108
Goldstein, Dora, 6
Goldstein, Lou, xvi, 41–43, *42, 43*, 45, 47, 52, *54*, 57–58, *57, 58*,

59, 61, 123, 125–26, 139, *179*, 184–85, 212
Goldstein, Philip, 6, 7
Goldy's Limousine Service, 96
Gomez, Lefty, 37
Gorme, Eydie, *163*, 193, 195
Goshen, New York, 13
Goulet, Robert, 152
Graham, Arnold, 87–88, 121, *193*
Grand Hotel, 130, 226
Grant, Cary, *159*
Green, Abel, 223
Greenberg, Henry, 39
Greenberg, Ralph, xvi, 122–23, 125
Greene, Shecky, 191
Greenfield Park, New York, 8, 10, 12, 19
Greenwald, Abraham, 142, 153
Greenwald, Joey, xvi, 142–44, 148, 153, 154–57, 158
Greenwald, Phil, *62–63, 71*, 108, 131, 153–60, *155, 157, 158*, 161, *161, 194*
Gregory, Dick, 166–67
Grey, Joel, 44, 191
Grillo, Frank, 135
Grine, Felder, 62, 64
Grossinger, Elaine, 30–31, *33–34*, 41, 47, 52, 54
Grossinger, Harry, 28–30, 31, *31, 32*, 33, 40, *45*, 46–47, *47*, 184, *209*
Grossinger, Jennie, 27, 28–30, *30*, 31, *31*, 32, *33–34*, 34, *36*, 39, 43–44, 47–49, *47–50*, 52, 59, 60, 194, 208, *208*
Grossinger, Karla, 43–44
Grossinger, Malke, 28, 32, 209, *209*
Grossinger, Paul, xvi, 28–31, 31, 34, *38*, 41, 42, *49*, 51, 54, 60, 61, 126, 144, 223
Grossinger, Selig, 28
Grossinger, Tania, xvi, 43–44, 46, 47, 54–55, 57, 59–60
Grossinger family, 1, 28, 43
Grossinger's Hotel, 1, 7, 11, 19, 27, 28–61, 81, *110*, 128, *136–37*, 144, 147, 151,

152, *179*, 191, *204*, 220
Concord versus, 151–52, 175
dancing at, 43, 47, 57, *96*, 135–36, 138–41
decline and sale of, 60–61, 225
food at, 204–6, 209–10, 223
Grossman, Irving, 70

H

Hackett, Buddy, 44, 71, *83*
Hagan, Cliff, 123
Halbert, Manny, 192, 219–20
Hall, Mike, xvi, 22, *26*, 219
Hampton, Lionel, xvi, 44, 44
Hanover, Norman, xvi, 110–12
Hardin's Farm, 17–18
Haring, Ernie, xvi, 35–36, 47–48, 206–7, 209–10, 220–21
Harmony Country Club, 24–25
Harold's employment agency, 216, 221
Hart, Moss, 1, 144
Hartman, Don, 50
Hawkins, Erskine, 154
Hayes, Peter Lind, *66*
Healy, Mary, *66*
Heiden Hotel, 214, 216, 232
Henry, Pat, 158
Hershon, Jerry, 196
Heston, Charlton, 139
Hill, Arthur, 6
Hill, John, 6
Hillig, Otto, 15, *15*
Hines, Hines, and Dad, 162–63
Hirschbein, Peretz, 62
Home National Bank, 8–9
Holder, Ma, 21, 23, 130
Holmes, Tommy, 45–46
Homowack Lodge, 182, 185
Hope, Bob, 193, *193*
Hopkins, Linda, xviii, 90, 108, 188, *189*
Horne, Lena, 164
Horner, Jackie, xvii, 43, *43*, 56–57, *96*, 135–38, 139–41, 204–6
Hotels:
    expansion of boardinghouses into, 7